CAT AND I

CAT AND I

DORIS SCHWERIN

LARGE PRINT BOOK CLUB EDITION

1817

HARPER & ROW, PUBLISHERS, New York

Grand Rapids, Philadelphia, St. Louis, San Francisco
London, Singapore, Sydney, Tokyo, Toronto

Quality Printing and Binding by:
ARCATA GRAPHICS/KINGSPORT
Press and Roller Streets
Kingsport, TN 37662 U.S.A.

FOR CHARLIE
(Charles Schlein, 1899–1988)

Contents

CONTENTS

HOME
IN THE CITY

The Will

MISS WILLOW was one hundred and twenty-six when she died. We had shared the same house for twenty-one years. I had lived longer with her than with my mother, who died when I was fourteen. I left my father's house when I was sixteen, to go to college. Not even our son was under our roof as long as Miss Willow was. Only Jules, my husband, has outdistanced her when it comes to the heavy-duty sharing of Time and Space—that consistent, unrelieved intimacy that can break or cement a love as it plows the days, seasons, years, even astrophysical changes as she was. To this day, I have not met anyone as sensitive to those changes. Sunspots, the vagaries of the jet stream, magnetic pulls, the auguries and patterns of the planets could startle her into a "What's that? What now?" —because her structure was a nexus to them all.

After her death, I was amazed to discover that she really had been attempting her autobiography, in the manner she had once told me: "I write in the air. . . ." There was no question about it—she was all around me in an indestructible, hieratic form . . . thoughts lingering in rooms, events described and hanging like clouds impossible to tear up, appearing, disappearing. And I was in shock. She had betrayed our years of intimacy by writing down pretty much everything that had passed between us.

There was her final wish, nervy as hell: "This, the story of my life thus far, in this body, will be typed by her, but every word has been conceived by me."

She had counted on my being able to decode her work, for one; but she also knew that if I didn't cause her airy *oeuvre* to materialize, I wouldn't be able to bear the guilt. She knew me well.

But I shall not do what she ordered; I will edit and expurgate, I think.

My hesitation reminds me of the fights we used to have about writing commercial. That gray, fluffy being could play an excoriating devil's advocate. She was fed up with my moanings and groanings and would mock: "You, with your repetition of patterns, your complaints about 'the rejection of the poetic' . . . fa! You, with your endless brouhahas over contracts, your intentions not being honored, and hovering over it all like an endless hot and humid wind is the specter of poverty. Boring, boring. When are you going to learn? Who knows better than I? I'm three inches away from you all day long!"

One day she offended me so, I didn't communicate with her for a whole day. "Do it or get off the pot," she had flung at me.

"Do what?"

"Knock out one of those sex, power, and money novels, like your agent wishes you would. It'll solve all our problems."

"You don't understand, I . . . it's a special craft, it's—"

With derision that felt like a knife, she began to quote from one of my poems: " 'Let us ferret out the single stem of passion.'/ 'It feels like murder in the garden.' "

On she went, with her relentless critique: "You got the right word—*passion*—but the wrong way. *Show* it, don't think about it; for *that,* there's an audience of ten!"

I flung back at her: "I am not a snob, I just can't do it!" I paused. "Are you a giraffe?"

"Obviously not; I'm a cat this Time around."

"Then you can't perform like a giraffe, no matter if, just once, you'd like the experience of nibbling leaves off the tops of trees! You can't, because you've got short little legs and you don't have a long neck; you're a preordained shape and limited, not necessarily diminished by a master plan. Of course money makes everything sweeter and calms the heartbeat. If I could, I would, just once, write a sex, power, and money novel, in my own way, damn it!"

Maybe she was only too right.

Why couldn't I write a linear, fast-forward, quick-to-the-car-chase-under-the-aqueduct - into - an - abandoned - warehouse, fight-for-your-life, kill-it push-it-over-the-ledge-fifty-feet-down-into-cement, a-body-lies-spread-eagled, a-murky-puddle-gets-an-infusion-of-blood-violence scene in the first ten pages?

While a woman waits in a motel, painting her toenails, her skin green in the off-and-on neons from the disco across the street. Waits for him—a serial killer. Only she doesn't know he's a serial killer; he's her brother-in-law. If only she knew that she was in love with a psychopath! It was bad enough to be waiting for an assignation with her sister's bull, enough guilt for any sibling to face the gods with. She would think like that because I would make her a professor of anthropology sunk into the seamy, gone bad, and would want to analyze why. . . . And there would go the whole thing for pages, there would go the required rhythms of white-knuckle, delicious-evil-gone-mad-with-de-sire-making-everyone-a-voyeur, instant-grat-ification writing out the window.

If I should want to texture the sunk-into-the-seamy tale, how could I get back on the track, to his hands encircling her neck, strangling her (because his mind had snapped from being so *serial)*, her mouth wide open and screaming? A woman screaming is money in the bank; so is titillating the male unconscious.

"Can't do it," I tried to explain to my colleague under the desk lamp. I thought she knew me well enough, but I was wrong. I had to remind her that I was out of sync, a throwback. The acme of a sex, passion, and the-wages-of-greed scene for me was still Emma Bovary dying in her suffocating nineteenth-century parlor, staring out the window at her neglected garden, a tiny, delicate, black spittle of death oozing from her pretty mouth. . . . Poor, longing bourgeois, dead from dreams and what she could never have: money, class, passionate, undying love fulfilled. And how brilliantly Flaubert had textured the story of Emma, fated her, sculpted her out of her society's historical space and time.

Was a writer only to make nightmares and leave it at that, for empty eyes and a shrug, a "Well, thank God, my life is better than that!" . . . then off with the lights to sleep and dream of nothing? Wasn't the sleight of hand expected of a writer to make dreams, too? There were some things I would not share with the presence on my desk, I decided.

The damn cat had opened up Pandora's box.

It is impossible to write of *hers* without writing of *mine*. She might have existed for me to attempt just *that*.

A Usual Day

As USUAL, she was sitting on the page I had just typed and put aside, her face tilted up to the lamplight, eyes half-closed in that sybaritic angle of pleasure, as if she were a sunbather at Palm Beach.

"Will you please remove yourself?" I ordered. "I can't see what I'm doing."

I knew I shouldn't have sounded testy, the minute the words were out of my mouth. She was annoyed but complied by moving herself a few inches off the page.

"Thank you, love," I responded graciously.

"Don't mention it." Willow turned from

the artificial sun to set her gaze on the bridge of my nose, intentionally avoiding my eyes. "Well, how's it going, may I ask?"

"You ought to know, you've been warming it up."

"Very amusing," she grunted.

"To answer your question, it doesn't please me."

"Nothing pleases you."

"Where on earth did you get that idea?"

She backed away. "Well . . . when you're working."

"It's a built-in occupational disease, honey, not feeling pleased moment to moment," I said.

"What a way to live! And don't use 'honey,' like your theatrical friends when they're nasty. I detest cheap irony."

Her nose twitched with irritation. Good lord, she was getting impossible in her old age!

"Do other writers behave the way you do, forehead all creased up?" she added. "Whatever you're working on has made a new horizontal line between your eyes. You better watch it, the way you worry with your face. What are they doing for wrinkles these days, collagen injections? Your actress friend mentioned it the other day, remember? She said she just had it done. *I* didn't see any difference, did you?"

"You know you can be very bitchy sometimes? To answer your question: Looking for the right way to say something causes uncertainty, momentary displeasure." (I felt the need to defend myself, because I do find the right way occasionally.) "Stop washing your rear end when I'm talking to you!"

"What are you angry about? I don't like being pushed!"

"I didn't push you."

"The tone of your voice did. What's the difference?"

"I don't like anyone looking down their nose at me when I'm working."

"Looking down *her* nose, not *their* nose, la-la," she corrected me gleefully.

"Oh, terrific." I reacted with disdain, but we both knew, when it came to that, I was never her equal. "Now, will you please get off my desk? You're disturbing me."

"You have no right to talk to me like that. I'm old enough to be your mother!"

I groaned and put my head in my hands.

Ordinarily she was an admirable companion, maybe even a steadying influence, but sometimes she would decide to be intrusive when I worked, even mocking, as if to test me. I should have been used to it, since she had done it for years.

This particular morning she knew I was foundering off a rocky coast, listing and drawing water, a craft about to be sucked down into the deep. I was looking for a connecting link between two paragraphs, a way to relate one time sequence to another, and was failing. She was on the boat with me and didn't like it. Would she have to jump off the deck and find a safer place to wash her tail? She knew all the signs: I was about to leave the sinking craft of a morning's work, exhausted, and go out for a walk. My leaving never appealed to her because she couldn't join me. That was not my fault. She had complained more than once after abortive attempts to take her out into the sun, that she was much too elegant to sit on my shoulder like a monkey.

I had said, "OK, stay inside by yourself, we're not Siamese twins joined at the head." She hated being left, but stuck to her guns when it came to city streets. She preferred the hothouse life, the artificial warmth of a hundred-watt bulb, the safety of the familiar, and stubbornly kept to her decision for years. The Long Island seashore and Vermont were other matters, both experiences filled with disaster for her, each of a different kind and with lifelong consequence.

"I don't understand," she said pityingly, "why it isn't a pleasure to write. I would adore it—nothing to do but sit there, plug your head into your heart, your heart to your fingers, your fingers to the machine, and let it fly! I would be a writer to reckon with, if I had fingers."

She was being successful in keeping me from leaving, of course. I had to respond to *that* one. "You'd never ask a writer 'How's it going?' if you had any notion about writing. Anything else is easier than words.

"Look at me! Don't turn away, you started this! Think of it, Willow, a painter has the comfort of canvas, paper, colors, sprays, brushes, oil, water. A sculptor has tools, metal, stone, wood, glass, wire, you name it. A dancer or a singer has a whole body of muscles to fall back on, plus music.

The musician? An instrument, something to hide behind, to hold, even to accept the blame if the weather is fickle. But the writer? Nothing but the unseen, the right and left brain functions, mysterious synapses, memory chips that no one knows anything about. . . ."

She was closing her eyes, telling me, "Enough, enough, I'm sorry." But I was not about to let her off. "A writer is also expected—or be damned—to be able to sing arias, sculpt bodies, paint interiors, exterior landscapes, dance stories across a stage that isn't there until the writer builds it, plank by plank. There's always the threat of a hidden precipice waiting, a headlong fall into a soundless room where you can go mad. . . ."

She opened her eyes. *"Mea culpa. . . .* Then why don't you forget about it?"

"Because you like milk and honey and kidney pie, and they cost money! Because I have things to say. That's unfair of you . . ."

"Say to whom? Who's waiting? Who's listening?" she asked.

"I don't need you this morning, thank you."

She looked at me with total wistfulness (her art of apology) and said, "You're my best friend this Time around. I do love you, you know."

It was a moment we had played many times together and it always left me weak, a moment she commanded with her beauty and she knew it. I answer with my eyes: Really? You love me?

She nods yes.

We are like two actors sitting at a bar, mouthing their favorite Shakespeare to each other every time they meet. I waited for her next line:

"Of course I love you. If you and he hadn't picked me out of the garbage can that night, I probably wouldn't have made it."

I laughed. She had drawn me out of anxious work space into a territory with no rational dimensions—when you look deep into the eyes of a cat, where the secrets of the universe siesta in dumb splendor.

Lest I be accused of anthropomorphism and talking animals: Who's to say there is no magic, no silent communication among all

living things, that coincidence is coincidental, or that the energies and soul sounds of
man and beast (maybe even flower, tree,
bush!) once activated, are not always alive?
Since no one has yet figured out what Time
is, much less Life and Death, who's to say
that we humans are the only ones whose fingers are nimble enough to fiddle around with
the combination of the cosmic lock?

She leaned toward me for a rare kiss. Our
noses touched, and her gorgeous opal eyes
cued me into: "You were the scraggliest little
gray thing, half in, half out of that rusty garbage can, with a week-old chicken bone in
your mouth. You were an unbelievable piece
of life."

But, unlike the scene we had played so
many times before, she began to improvise,
first with a sigh: "Emaciated, dehydrated,
and raped at the age of six months."

"I didn't know you had that kind of memory!"

"Well, it's not like yours. I have the ad-
vantage of a small brain—no room for the
extraneous, the unresolved, misconceptions,
the talent to waver. It's a blessing. My brain
has room only for the significant. I write,

too, you know, not the way you do, though.
I don't make such a production out of it. I
write in the air; it just hangs there, it's always there. Haven't you ever noticed? For
instance, I've written about that night you
and he found me." She threw her head back
and began to recite:

It was a snowy night and I felt quite near
death. I had crawled up from that
miserable cellar to find some food. I
smelled. I was too weak to wash myself.
You couldn't tell what color I was, and I
still hadn't gotten over being raped by a
huge form that had come up from behind
me, out of the shadows. A spiky rod had
gone into me like fire and my back was
bitten. I screamed until I thought my eyes
would fall out. Afterward I just lay there
whimpering near the boiler in that terrible
cellar. I had no idea what anything meant,
I was too young. . . .

She stopped, yawned, found an imaginary
itch to scratch, and then looked at me. "I've
never said this before, but I do not like being
enclosed in the form of a cat." Whereupon

she clamped her little mouth shut, closed her eyes, and resumed her sunbathing under the heat of the Palm Beach lamp.

She was waiting for me to react. With neck arched, shoulders back, every hair and muscle alert to the fact that no aristocratic symmetry could match hers at that moment, she waited.

It must have been the perfect white star on her forehead, her tiny white feet in a perfect ballet fifth position, as if a god-choreographer had so placed them, that made me suddenly remember a conversation Joseph Conrad had written between a rare-butterfly collector and his friend. I got up to find the book and read the passage out loud to myself:

The collector was showing his friend a most rare specimen of butterfly, commenting, "Marvelous! Look! The beauty—but that is nothing—look at the accuracy, the harmony. And so fragile! And so strong! And so exact! This is Nature—the balance of colossal forces. Every star is so—and every blade of grass is so—and the mighty Kosmos in perfect equilibrium produces—this. This wonder; this masterpiece of Nature—the

great artist?" The visitor responded to his
entomologist-friend: "Masterpiece! And
what of man?" The entomologist answered:
"Man is amazing, but he is not a masterpiece! Eh? What do you think? Sometimes it
seems to me that man is come where he is
not wanted, where there is no place for him;
for if not, why should he want all of the
place? Why should he run about here and
there making a great noise about himself,
talking about the stars, disturbing the blades
of grass?"

Willow opened her incredible opal eyes,
with their long, white, cobwebby lashes.
. . . "Not bad, especially the 'making a
great noise about himself.' But to get back to
what I was saying before: When I said 'I was
too young,' I meant—I thought that's what I
was put on this earth for, to be raped when
ready."

It was as if I had been suddenly stung by
an errant bee blown miles and years away
from its native garden. I reeled backward.

I am fifteen. On the stage of a Boston concert hall and performing as the accompanist-
composer for a modern dance recital.

Dressed in a robin's-egg-blue gown, my
dark, long, shiny hair à la Veronica Lake
(the hair taking care of it all, half-hiding the
face, adolescent blemish, psychopathic shyness, sexual hysteria, and a thin, prominent
nose), my feet under the voluminous skirt
trembled on the piano and forte pedals as if I
were a patient undergoing shock treatment.

The concert has just finished, but the
quaking child at the piano must have given
off waves of *something,* like passion, talent,
the Lady of the Camellias or the Lake,
mixed well with Venus rising out of her sea-
shell. In those tender years I worked myself
senseless in front of the bathroom mirror for
that combination of unavailability and al-
lure. (I suspect I still do, but with the laugh
of an aging virago.) For a young music critic
rose from his seat, walked onstage, and introduced himself. He took my icy hands in
his, told me how talented I was, and invited
me out for a drink.

A drink? He must think me a woman of
the world, sixteen at least. And he wasn't
short, pasty-faced, pig-eyed, and goggled. He
was taller than I, who had always been the
second-tallest girl in class, ever since the fifth

grade. He was curly-blond, square-cheeked, full-lipped, with serious blue eyes that had the most incredibly long lashes I had ever seen. The young critic pronounced, "You're wonderful."

Finally, a man, not a boy! Every handsome stranger who had ever walked across the pages of dog-eared library books read by flashlight was holding my cold hands in his. Flush, sweat, moistness. Whatever was happening to me had never happened before. My glands had taken over, secreting moon juice.

Sitting across from me at a table in an Austro-Hungarian restaurant, with soft waltzes playing and wreaths of fake flowers looped around everything that didn't move, he deduced immediately that I had no idea what drink I wanted, much less how to call it, so he ordered a claret lemonade for me and scotch for himself, and I think we talked about music. I don't think I knew *then* what we talked about; I became instantly dizzy on the claret and was aware of nothing but his eyes. I had never looked *into* the eyes of a grown man before. We must have been talking about music, because at one point he clapped his hands and cried, "Composer! Composer!"

The man must be mad, of course. Couldn't he see that I was still an amoeba squirming around in the mud? But suddenly the most miserable year of my life, in a fog of loneliness, confusion, and unacknowledged mourning—the year after my mother died— was coming to an end. Because of music and a stranger. I not only had accompanied the dancers in the concert but also had written two compositions for the event and was going to be reviewed. Maybe he was right; maybe I *was* promising, talented, the Camellia lady pasted onto Venus, paper dolls come alive. After all, he should know; he was twenty-two, he said. It was amazing to look into his eyes and see in them the quintessential woman that my mirror had always assured me was there.

A generation later I sit looking into a cat's eyes, their unwavering, challenging stare impossible to ignore or break. She sits there, a furry plumb line, perfectly centered, ears pointed to the heavens, breathing from her vagina (following all the musts of Martha

Graham for the perfect dancer, female *or* male.) Dance: one of the most ancient forms of magic. Willow sits there, a miniature Easter Island stone, daring me to exhume a secret, then dance with the cadaver of my virginity.

OK, lady, I thought. He wrote me love letters signed in blood, but I thought he was the sanest person in the world because he said he loved me. I was amazed to be wanted. He pursued me right down to a summer afternoon, right into my bedroom at home, not the backseat of a car or under a tree . . . right into the room where I had had chicken pox, Mama and Papa coming in to comfort; the same white, pristine, waffled counterpane. (Mama always called my bedspread "counterpane," in honor of Robert Louis Stevenson's poem she read to me when I was sick . . . "When I lay sick a-bed," or something like that. I was not going to get up and check it out, as I had the Conrad; Willow was keeping me much too busy.)

In that room with the smell of summer behind the drawn blinds, I was being made love to and wasn't ready. It couldn't be love! His blue eyes with their long lashes had

turned wild. Everything about him, his
mouth, flaring nostrils, stocky body, blond
curly hair, pressed down on me and I gasped
for breath, terrified. What is this? This is *it?*
The *it* my friend Roxanne and I giggled
about behind stone fences? This was no giggling matter. A demanding stranger with a
hairless tail rams it, pushes, searches impatiently for a door, breaks down the hinges,
they bleed and give in as it races downward,
sideways, slamming against the walls of a
bottomless cave, a startling, anatomical
space I never knew I had.

It couldn't be love. I scream "No! I can't
breathe! Stop!" He doesn't listen. The other
screams were silent ones. I was too overwhelmed with guilt . . . invasion . . .
pain . . . amazed by the rite of passage.
Rape. I knew it in my dumbness. Years later,
the dumbness bursts like heavy water and
rains down in a fury. I was trying to reach
out to the girl on the bed, trying to make out
the words behind her eyes. Shame, disap-
pointment, shock, sadness, and that peculiar
sense of pride, because she was no longer a
girl but a woman, *no matter the horror.*
(There are myriad shades of violence de-

nied.) She was a girl in a time of no audible
female outrage. I reached out my arms to
calm her and tell her an astounding prophecy: She would live to straddle changing
times, like others had lived between candle
and gas, between sail and steam. There
would come a day when the female No!
would no longer be kept inside.

"You humans with your memory chips,"
the presence on my desk crooned, not to me
but to the hundred-watt bulb. She was purring so, I knew she had picked up the trans-
missions. "You're at it again," she whistled
through her teeth. "You're taking all the air
out of the room."

"Oh, shut up, you started it, with your
rape in the cellar next to the boiler!"

"It was just a commercial way to begin
my autobiography—how it is to be a cat,
though a little young, in my case." She
paused. "But in your case, *was* it rape? You
make such a big deal out of everything. Want
to talk about it? Was there mutual consent?
The truth, now—"

I couldn't believe it, I was answering. "I
was too scared, ignorant, and honored to say
no."

"The truth, now. . . . Were you caressed and aroused before the invasion? That's the way of humans, isn't it?"

"It wasn't that way."

"Did he bite your back?"

"No!"

"Stop yelling!"

"I'm not yelling!"

"Did you complain that you were being hurt?"

"I tried. He stopped for a second, with a funny, uncomprehending look, then he began again with even more resolve. But yes, he ignored my terror."

"More truth. Did you feel attraction, love in spite of the pain?"

"No." I closed my eyes to remember. "I just remember his weight, Your Honor, his will. I didn't know the phrase then, but I felt it—his biological imperative that had to be obeyed."

"It was rape," she pronounced solemnly. "Well, how about that! How come you never told me? Join the club."

I finally got myself up from the desk. "Yes, little one, like most women from way back in the caves, to the medieval ghettos and castles, to the Victorian tenements and mansions, to the split-level ranch houses with the two-car garages. Until a minute away from yesterday, the female no was silent, with exceptions, of course. How shocking to think that I wasn't an exception. And I don't want to talk about it anymore."

Sometimes she almost did seem like my mother back again, a demanding, multi-antennaed perfectionist from whom no secrets could be hidden, or the freaked-out mother of a pharaoh, a dusty, exasperated spirit laden with astral wisdom that no one wanted to heed even *before* she was mummified.

I left her sitting under the lamp with her mouth open. I was not about to share with her what was roiling around in my head, about what she referred to as *your species,* with its big brain, mass unconscious, and a miasma of memory. It has no predator but itself, so it had to invent guilt, the cross, Commandments, fables, allegories, bibles, philosophers, poets—to coerce itself away from evil, into gentleness and love. Yet none of it stops the Furies from bursting out, again, again in a bedroom, a street. A whole country of the species can explode into gang-bang torture, bestiality, the rape of war. The sexuality of power and death is deliciously chilling to my species.

I locked up the apartment to go for a walk. I could hear her meowing behind the door, the meows turning into yowls of annoyance at being left, not only alone but also in the middle of a rejoinder.

Friendship

SOME FRIENDSHIPS give off sparks enough to last a lifetime and beyond. You have but to open the drawer and there they are!—still sparkling, quivering with energized spiritual quarks. There is one that glints like onyx, my friend Charlotte, the painter, with her jet-black hair, working in her white studio to find some new, hard-edged visual poetry on canvas. There is another that hums like an emerald, my sister Elizabeth, the dancer. There is another that glitters like a cracked diamond, my high-school friend Roxanne. *And then there is Miss Willow.*

But first about Roxanne. Because, there she is, flashing, evoking the youthful days . . .

We both went off to college. We came home and walked together on the North Shore Massachusetts beaches, the long ribbons of sand between Essex and Gloucester, or the thin, rocky excuses for beach between Marblehead and Beverly—the authentic New England kind—chary, practical strips below the Calvinist rockbound coast.

And as we talked, comparing notes, we picked up sea-polished sticks in the form of wishbones, the canes of old men; giving them to each other as talismans to honor ourselves; it was the time to be arrogant as well as profligate, about Time. We were squirrels chattering about the butternuts, the choice little meats of life we had nosed into, grabbed for our own out there in the world. Which to crack and devour, which to put aside and save in the hole of a special tree? The floor of the forest was fecund with experiences we had each found and shared. Then our lives diverged both in pattern and place.

I had not seen Roxanne for years, when I

was informed that she had died. Our habit had been to visit by telephone at least twice a year. If there was a crisis, and Roxanne had had her share of them, it was more. There was that voice down through the years, so important and familiar that it overcame the physical vacuum with her first word.

As if it were as much a part of me as my fingerprints, there was her voice: twitchy, brilliant, sarcastic, self-examining, denigrating, loving, calling up our adolescence. Riding bicycles under the elms, we had practiced the art of obscenities like *turd, shit, bastard* in those innocent days before the revival of the Marquis de Sade's kink was added to the drug-cool, angry expletives of the oppressed and became common speech for even the nice and advantaged. Her voice could call up such virginal other times . . . giggling against stone fences, sharing the secrets of smoking, bleeding, and sex, as if they were the Devil's work, and other secrets to unfold, if only we could wait for life to unroll its magic carpet and the perfect male to come tumbling out.

What did unfold was life—with surprise, tragedy, shock, and more pleasure for me

than her. Through it all, we shared via
phone what had happened, the twists and
turns self-imposed or superimposed by others . . . and always with that laugh of hers,
straining to connect with God. Roxanne was
an unwavering Catholic, an alcoholic re-
formed or fallen, depending upon what year
it was, what mountain she had tried to climb
or turn back down from.

When I married, she sent me eight gleaming, handhewn mahogany plates from Peru,
where she was working as a governess the
year after she graduated from Wellesley College.

"You know what travel is supposed to
do," she bantered with her usual self-mock-
ing. "But I do love trains, those little swaying wombs chug-chugging down the track.
The thing about trains is"—she giggled—
"when you board them, everything is on
hold; it's good-bye to all the dreadful little
problems, you're free! That is, until you
reach your station and have to get off! And
there you are, and there they are, the little
orphans, waving their arms, waiting for you
to take care of them *the right way* this time."

Her giggle was the top of the iceberg,

straining against the restrictions of her Catholic guilt, her chastity belt. I think she died a virgin, that sophisticated, insatiable reader, probing, nervous, stylish, hard-drinking, brilliant-tongued, bitter, gentle woman. In one of her more desperate times, probably when she reached forty, she pleaded her way into being accepted as a novitiate in a Carmelite convent; the most punitive of orders was her choice.

She called me hurriedly, to tell me what she had done and that she would be "disconnected for a long time, darling, incommunicado."

I wrote her a short letter:

To my dear friend who has fled us in search of Grace:

Dearest Childhood, I can't imagine your middle-aged feet *discalced* [she also had very shapely legs], pattering on the cold Carmelite stone floors. Why, you were the first to wear heels! the first to use lipstick! to smoke! The first courageous one to be "naughty," lift a glass of *vino* and toast: "Here's to the prickly-pear time

when Fate is the body, God help us!" I
just can't imagine your tongue silent in
your mouth stuffed with a vow of silence.
Not when I remember our screaming out
our love, on our bicycles under the trees—
we made the afternoons cower from our
glorious idiocies. I can't believe you've
gagged your sense of humor. Barefoot and
silent, indeed! Think it over, friend. I
mean, how long do you people have to
keep yourself and That Poor Man on the
cross and bleeding, perpetuate that terrible agony? That isn't what He meant! Live
in the world to the fullest, loving and forgiving and changing, is what He meant.
Not disconnection and silence. For God's
sake, Jesus was a shouter, a singer.

I never mailed the letter, I was talking to
myself, but I was right about Roxanne, at
least. She lasted in the Carmelite convent for
six months or so, and was released by very
mutual agreement.

"My knobby knees just couldn't take the
kneeling, and my complaining, secular little
brain was very distraught with the endless
pot-scrubbing in the kitchen, even if beauti-

ful Mother Mary in all Her Grace seemed to be there, observing closer than I've ever felt her. . . . But, my dear, one of Mary's eyebrows was raised and I got the message. So did the Mother Superior!" Roxanne laughed, with acid in her tone, and—I could hear—warm with a few drinks. "So, that's that, for *that* road toward Redemption. Life is now saying, 'Where were we before we were interrupted, pussycat?' "

She sounded frightened and shaky behind the levity, but after that she was able to come to terms with herself for long spaces of time. After a particularly destructive bout with drinking, she went West, dried herself out, and worked in a drug-addict rehabilitation center for many years. She reported that she almost felt "at home, because the seashore of Puget Sound can *almost* be New England, if I close my eyes."

But behind her voice I could always hear: Remember how we used to toss our heads like young mares and flush our cheeks planning for the perfect love, the perfect work to make the world stand up and yell "Bravo!" and "Those women, how marvelous!"? Tell me what happened, her voice said underneath, in the bubbling river-sound of young days, in whose sunny afternoons under the trees Roxanne was planning to outshine Dorothy Parker as America's leading female, tragic-humorist writer. I wanted Igor Stravinsky to die so that his spirit would choose to inhabit my body, and together we would write the most incredible symphonies the world had ever heard. The witchery and hilarity of the youthful days and dreams quiver and sparkle in a second, they and Roxanne, when I open the drawer.

I think of my friendship with Miss Willow as made of marcasite set in silver. Its hibernation has turned the silver to gray, but the subtle steel facets still glint like tiny pieces of a shattered moon.

Miss Willow. My constant companion and colleague in my so-called maturity, when I arrived at a surprising crossroad where one could be called an *elder*. Definition: someone who must have accumulated a bit of wisdom along the way, or what's the point? And where life finally appeared more related, in shape, to a chambered nautilus pried open than to any other of nature's forms: a whorl of opalescent canyons sweeping downward clockwise, then up, up around the dizzying curve of memory, to the inevitable center of the shell—the heart.

Rescue

THE RUN-DOWN East European neighborhood of the East Village where we found Willow, with its Russian baths and Orthodox Church, was hanging on for dear life in the 1960s against the waves of beats and love children, the slow trickle-down of drugs from Harlem, and the wave of West Village people like us—artists, writers and musicians who saw in it a new Village with cheaper rent.

Still, ancient Ukrainian and Polish women in their flowered headscarfs, black dresses, vintage laced-up boots as wrinkled from life as their wearers, sat catching the sun in the park called Tompkins Square, and tenaciously protecting what was theirs, the decaying houses to the south and west of the park, or the tenements on the side streets.

In the early part of the century, the northern and eastern brownstones that faced the park used to be called Doctors' Row, the Park Avenue of the Lower East Side. Now, artists were moving in with their wooden shutters, geranium plants and grape ivy in window boxes, and brass knockers on the front doors, to announce: Genteel poverty, college educations, and/or aesthetic sensibilities have arrived to transform the fallen. The neighborhood stores, geared to immigrant needs for years, were flourishing as the new population discovered the joys of kielbasa, borscht, piroshki, the heavy hams and incredible breads that the old ladies in their black dresses insisted on. The East Village was a rich brew of the old and new. There seemed to be a conscious, if wary, pact by all parties to live curious about one another, but in peace. Best of all was the park's quadrangle, with its one-hundred-year-old trees, a rara avis in the city—you could see the sky from your windows! No towering coops yet, in the 1960s, to block out the seasons in the stone city.

I was born in a cellar in the East Village, New York City, surrounded by Ukrainian and Polish cats. I never felt Russian, not even when I was too young to know how I felt.

I'm sure I heard French and Tchaikovsky in my genes; they seemed so familiar to me later on. So I assume I'm Polish, from Warsaw, the Paris of the East. I was not descended from peasant village cats.

If you are born in a cellar, no place is a good place. Don't talk to me about immigrants; their cellars are filthy. Their landlords insist on filth just to let everyone know who's who and what's what.

I will never forget the hunger, the smells, the poverty of the lower depths. The psychosis of poverty would be behind my eyes for the rest of my life, if I lived to have another life.

How could we pass it by, make believe we didn't see it—a little one in dire trouble, to be rescued? Would we have dared to think twice if it had been a human infant? Maybe the only reason for your existence was to be walking down a snowy street at midnight and face damnation forever *if you didn't stop.*

Whatever we sensed, Jules and I, in that tiny, abject, flickering spirit of a kitten (aside from a spooky there-but-for-the-Grace-of-God-go-I feeling, and the cuckoo-idity of cat-lovers) she would later verify in her own words.

We had no choice but to extricate the emaciated little body from the garbage can and take her home, to give it and ourselves *reason.* At least until the next day, when there would definitely be second thoughts about saintly acts or the possibility of reincarnation and finding ourselves in the same position someday, not to mention the teachings of the elusive god-forces. All of it was wrapped up in one little victim of the flows of destiny—for the first few moments, anyway.

This life of hunger, punishment, and degradation must be payments for acts in

the dim past. There I was, innocent again,
too young to know about the Great Design
of reappearing, learning, refining, but there
I was! And there they were! I was close to
dying. What reason to live this life? I
challenged them: *You* tell me!

They placed me on a white bath mat
next to a warm steam pipe, wiped off my
fur, heated some milk in a little yellow pot,
and put it before me in a blue and white
saucer rimmed with gold. He did it,
actually, because she said, if I remember
correctly: "You do it. I'm wiped out just
with the thought of it. We need another
one like a hole in the head." Then she said,
"What? Are you using a Rosenthal plate?"

I shall never forget that moment as long
as I live. I went to sleep drugged, a sleep
without fear for the first time in my life.

The next morning I knew I had to
behave like a miracle, though I had to *wet*
so much, I thought I would burst. (I later
learned the word was *pee.)*

I didn't dare investigate where I was, for
fear I would leak, so I just sat there on the
white mat, looking up at them as they
looked down on me. How long could I

hold it? was making me as nervous as their talk about what to do with me, take me back to where they found me, or to an "animal shelter" where, she said, "they most certainly will put it down. There are too many kittens in the world to think they might clean up this one for adoption, and it's in terrible shape. Oh, God, look at that delicate face, it looks like a she and it's gray, like Willow was." I remember every word she said, and the look on her face when she said "Willow."

Suddenly he said he was going to the store and rushed out. While he was gone, I just sat there looking up at her and she looking down at me—eye to eye. I didn't look away once, because something was happening in her eyes—they were wetting and filled with words.

Back he came with a pan and what looked like rough sand in a bag. "Will it get the message?" he said.

Did I know what to do? I'd show them. They lifted me into the pan filled with sand and I let out a waterfall, pawed the sand over it carefully, then just as carefully stepped out, back to the white mat.

I knew those moments were crucial because something was telling me what to do. "Stay on that rug," it said. "Make a picture of irresistible pathos. Keep looking at them deep and long without blinking. Your death is imminent if they don't let you stay."

I began to tremble. If they didn't keep me in this warm, pretty place, so different from the rust-bleeding pipes and stinking filth of the cellar floor, I was going to be denied another Time around. I'd have to go back to the beginning, and who knew what that could be? Maybe plankton!

I didn't know then, but I know now that it was the Absolute Peaceful Hand talking to me, telling me what to do.

A Cat, a Dog, an Aunt

THE DECISION to keep her, invite her to stay being more to the point when it comes to cats, was not made entirely because of cosmic guilt. There were other reasons, which had nothing to do with the tiny gray orphan with incredible opal eyes.

We had had another gray cat the year before and her name was Willow. She was acquired to make up for a big loss—a beagle we had bought in a pet shop, pedigree and all, the year before Willow I.

What had happened to both the first gray cat and the dog, Peppy, led to yet another gray cat sitting before us on the white bath mat. The irony of the circumstance pushed us into the decision, as if our brains were made of milkweed and the winds of Fate had decided to blow.

Our first glimpse of Peppy was in a pet shop cage filled with squirming puppies, anarchy itself, tails and ears and sleek little behinds in perpetual motion. All except one, the runt of the litter sitting on shaky haunches in bewilderment, a sight certain to create an instant meltdown. That was Peppy, the weak one pushed aside and ignored, with the sweet, wistful, despairing face to go with it. He was our choice for our little boy, Chucky, of course, because I cry at Independence Day parades, root for the meek to inherit the earth, want dignity for the forgotten—the underdog.

Underdog, indeed! By the time Peppy was a year old he was huge, ugly-tempered, and untrainable, and thought that all problems could be solved by biting. We suffered his behavior patiently, trusting he could be loved out of his misconceptions. Peppy wasn't what you'd call the perfect dog for a little boy. We suffered Peppy's truancy until one day, at dinner, he jumped up and stole

Jules's meat right off his plate and began to devour it under the table.

Outraged, Jules crawled under the table to retrieve his dinner. Man and beast battled over the gravy-laden roast in a mad scramble, until Jules yelled in pain, "He's bitten my arm! That's it with this animal!" Peppy slunk off on his belly, his ears at half mast and huge beagle eyes brimming with guilt, but all the body English of a sinner couldn't help him this one-time-too-many. Jules emerged from under the table bleeding and pronounced, "If he doesn't know who his friend is by now, his time is up as far as I'm concerned."

"What does Daddy mean 'His time is up'?" Chucky asked. He was a dear little boy with huge brown eyes and a levelheadedness, even at the age of five, that neither of his parents possessed. He was also born with a fully developed sense of humor, and two cowlicks always standing up straight in his light brown hair glinting with red, giving him an air of expectancy, everything at the ready to ingest the wonders of the world. What had just happened wasn't one of the wonders.

Jules and I had talked about it privately, so we were almost ready when we tried to explain that some beagles can be miserable cooped up in a city apartment, because it was in their genes to be hunters, some more than others. Then had to follow the exploration of a new word: *genes.* So . . . Chucky could see that it was unfair for Peppy to live with us, even though we loved him and he thought he loved us. It did seem as if Peppy was one of those beagles born to live out in the open and hunt, and he was telling us in the only way he could, with his bad temper and biting. We would find a wonderful place for him to grow up and do what would make him happy. We almost believed what we were saying: understanding in the face of a mistake that could be rectified; it's the best of all possible worlds in the long run; wrongness could be transformed to rightness. It was the cornerstone of idealism; one owed that to a child of five. But in the back of our heads was: Never adopt an animal from a pet shop unless you know the owner *and* the breeder. Unless you're prepared to run a rehabilitation center for nature's traumatized or sports.

We called some fishermen-duck hunters we knew on Long Island and offered them a pedigreed beagle. They were delighted. Apprised of the biting eccentricity, they said not to worry, they'd train him, shape him up, and he could run the marshes to his heart's content.

Several years later we had occasion to meet the fishermen on a walk down a beach. "How's the dog, Peppy?" we asked. The fishermen laughed. "That dog? He's a bad one, born bad." Did they still have him? we asked, hoping Chucky, at our side, wouldn't be distressed. "Do we have him? We sure do. He's as big as a house, a mean whale of a critter, has to be chained most of the time, but oh, can he hunt when the duck season comes around. He's a winner!"

Shortly after we had given Peppy to the fishermen, we adopted a little gray cat from the ASPCA. She was a gem of a creature, and we named her Willow. She could be hugged by a little boy, with impunity; there were no ducks floating in front of her eyes, no wild grass or shadows to throttle to death.

* * *

The first Willow was with us no more than a few months when an inconceivable horror took place. My father's older sister, Aunt Edys, a kindly, handsome lady in her seventies, was murdered by a psychopath known as the Boston Strangler. She was one of his many victims who lived in the Beacon Hill area of Boston and had opened her door to him on a Sunday afternoon.

Such tragedy only happens to other families, unfortunate strangers dragged wild-eyed and weeping onto the front page. He had robbed her, trussed her up, raped her, then strangled her to death. My father, a doctor in Peabody, eighteen miles away, was informed either by the Boston police or a neighbor, he couldn't remember which, but he drove the eighteen miles so fast, he arrived at the scene even before a Boston doctor or an ambulance. Poor man, he was the first expert to view the carnage in his sister's apartment. There is no doubt in my mind that it shortened his own life. He said that in all his years of practicing medicine, he had never witnessed such physical abomination, and that included devastating automobile accidents. He refused to tell us what he saw.

Only after much time had passed did he say once, "Terrible things had been done with a broom."

We brought Chucky to my sister, Elizabeth, and her son, Peter, four years older then Chucky and his favorite person. She would take care of the kids and we would run to help Papa. We left little Willow with the nearest vet who boarded animals in the Village, and caught the first train to Boston, where a cousin would meet us. At the station we were greeted by three-inch headlines screaming out the death of my aunt, and we had the most peculiar reaction—embarrassed laughter of disbelief, and then the kind of anger that bursts blood vessels. There was still the eighteen-mile drive north to Peabody, to see Papa's face.

It was a surprise. Papa had been weaned in Tsarist Russia, on the tenebrous masterpieces of Gogol, Dostoyevski, Gorky, pogroms, and violence, especially at Christmas and on Easter Sunday; the Russian peasants, on their highest holy days, loved to get on horseback, rape and ravage through the Jewish part of a village, to remind the Jews that they had murdered Christ. Now my father, the sophisticated healer, the intellectual, had set his face unmoved, maybe even curious. His sister's death was yet another event in Man's inhumanity and madness, to be analyzed. Otherwise he couldn't have sustained the realization of her murder and the funeral to come. But underneath, the stab of the Devil's knife had rent his soul, the Devil in the guise of the Boston Strangler.

Lives are like chairs: Some are tufted and gimped more richly, some stiff and plumped up because they sit in shadowy corners, unused; some hide broken springs, clotted balls of stuffing—the secrets of years covered and re-covered by fancy fabric. Some lives are hard wooden chairs indented by years of body weight, smoothed by the touch of hands. My aunt's life was a Shaker chair, proudly made, pure of line, free of pretense, its intention nakedly clear: *to be of use.* Her life had been dedicated to the nurturing of a son and his promise.

My father had helped to extricate her, a young widow, and her little boy of two, as well as his old mother and a younger sister, from Russia. If Papa, wild, rebellious, and radical when he was a teenager, had stayed in his Ukrainian town, he would have been hanged, like some of his friends were later in the town square. He came to America alone, put himself through high school, college, medical school, and internship, married a beautiful nurse with similar radical leanings, and became the first Jewish doctor in a Yankee town. My Aunt Edys arrived in America when Elizabeth was six, the year I was born.

Grandmother, aunts and cousins settled in Boston. Aunt Ronnie, the youngest of my father's siblings (the rest were murdered by either the Germans or the Russians), half blind, sickly from years of bouts with tuberculosis (she was almost turned back at Ellis Island), eventually married. Aunt Edys, blond and handsome, never remarried. She worked in a factory for most of her life, and with the help of Grandmother guarded a nest so that a young boy showing the signs of the gifted could grow and flower. He plowed his way through school, college, advanced degrees from M.I.T., and became his mother's dream fulfilled, a man of value, a scientist.

When the Boston Strangler, in the guise of a repairman, climbed the stairs to my aunt's apartment on a Sunday afternoon, she was a retired old lady living alone, enjoying her walks along the Charles River, hours of earned ease and pride. She need never be used again, except to be admired.

She was to be buried in the family plot in Peabody. Her son, arriving from New Jersey, knew only what Papa had dared tell him on the phone: "Come quickly, your mother is dying; I've taken her to Peabody." And Papa hung up, unable to say more. My cousin didn't call back, he didn't press his uncle for details. Ours was a very formal family. If his revered Uncle Harry chose to withhold information, he'd have to wait for the particulars. My cousin worried all the way to Boston. What was it, a heart attack, a stroke? So formal, so independent, he didn't tell anyone how or what time he was coming, or he would have been met. On the bus (of all ways!) from Boston to Peabody, my cousin looked over the shoulder of a man reading a newspaper and saw "Beacon Hill Widow Murdered!" and learned that it was his mother.

My cousin had a reputation for having studied and worked with the chemical Lithium especially its tranquilizing properties. The day of the funeral, distraught and torn from his moorings, he hissed a confidence to Jules: He was so angry he wanted to kill, and he was going to. The Pentagon and the Defense Department had approached him to work on a chemical warfare project, top secret. He had refused the offer with an emphatic no, but now he was going to call them back and say yes! He wanted his work to kill. Jules tried to calm him, it was understandable that he should feel that way on such a day, but he had better consult a psychiatrist when the shock of his mother's death had subsided, before he made a decision about germ warfare.

How much cruelty can the rational tolerate before they become the enemy's echo? Only reason can heal. Revenge is not sweet; it's bitterness riding a rocket to hell. My cousin did not reconsider the Pentagon's offer, though it was impossible for him to forget that his mother went "raging" into that good afternoon. She must have fought like a lioness, the police told him, because of the upheaval in her apartment. One detective made a strange, touching comment, the comment of a simple working man trying to give balm to a bereaved son: "You know, there wasn't a speck of dust under your mother's bed."

Detectives would attend the funeral as mourners, we were notified, because "Sometimes the killer likes to come to his victim's funeral." The police asked Jules if he would alert them to any strangers, since he seemed to be the only family member with his wits about him. Jules agreed to help, though he knew no one in the cemetery except the immediate family, and few of them. Everyone looked like a stranger. How do you tell a dangerous stranger? The detectives came up to him: What about that one, this one? Do you know him? Jules skulked around with a Groucho Marx crouch inside his head, appalled by the yardstick he had decided to use: Who's Jewish? The Strangler couldn't be a Jew! How do you tell a Jew? Long sideburns, a black fur hat, a crooked nose, curly black hair? A yellow star? Papa's family were fair-haired and blue-eyed, a middleclass family that had fled from Germany to the Ukraine during the Peasant Revolution of 1847. I remember my Aunt Edys when I was small—with her fair hair, peachy skin, and glistening blond braids wound about her head.

Now she was being lowered, in a body bag inside a coffin, an old lady abominated beyond recognition.

The madman had not chosen to be present. It was raining.

When we got back to New York, we retrieved the children. First, Chucky from his Aunt Elizabeth's. He had had a fine time, though Elizabeth had found it difficult to contain her distress about what was going on in Peabody. The children were not to know the reason we went "to see Grampy," not until they were old enough to deal with lurking insanity.

Willow did not have a fine time. She had caught something from one of the other animals at the vet's. We nursed a sorry bit of fluff for a week, and Willow died of cat enteritis. Another lesson learned the hard way: Don't *ever* leave a healthy animal at a vet's unless you know the owner!

A year of disaster, with a dog, an aunt, a cat. Enough was enough. No more pets. At least we could spare ourselves *that* investment in love and death.

Yet there we were, six months later, plucking a little cat out of the garbage. "How can we leave it? It's gray! Another Willow!"

And so the second Willow joined us for a very long time. The decision was as loaded with portent and pastent as a Homeric tale. Little did she know. . . . Or did she?

Births and
Beginnings

LOOK WHAT SHE IS! Beautiful.

Willow II. We called her Miss Willow, to make the distinction between I and II. She began to glisten silver-gray as she became strong enough to wash herself. All gray, except for the white cross on her forehead and tiny white paws, everything about her was delicately balanced; she was a miniature beauty, aristocracy of form, a cameo cat . . . and we figured about six months old. The clincher was her eyes: wide opal orbs lidded with strangely long, white, cobwebby lashes, which she blinked mercilessly in her own behalf.

We wanted no mistakes with her, only the best. She was brought to the finest cat doctor in the city. After inoculating her, palpating and probing, he stood back and announced: "She's pregnant."

In no time at all, we had five cats.

The delicately constructed one, an adolescent herself, performed her motherly duties with the strength of a full-bosomed, fearless matriarch easy and familiar with the mysteries of Nature's prime demand of her. Her little body had milk enough for all; she washed her kittens until she fell back in exhaustion, without a complaint. Ah, but the way she related to her children was ridiculously human, from unfair and cruel to overweaning. She was impatient, disdainful of Twinky, the runt of the litter, as much as she tried to hide it. She adored Blacky, jet-black and arrogant, the only male of the litter, and she spoiled him outrageously (my son, the doctor). Missey, as beautiful as her mother, Willow admired and washed her face constantly. But Patches, an adorable motley-colored little peasant of jumbled black, white, and tan—probably inherited from her ox of a father—Willow felt needed nothing but food. We kept putting Patches in front of her for that little bit of affection so crucial for self-confidence, but Willow would have none of her. Patches must have reminded her of that monster in the cellar.

When the time came for kitten school, Willow turned into a thin-lipped, exacting teacher insisting on excellence. She lined up her four kittens a few feet away from the litter pan. They sat at attention, eight wide-open eyes, ears cocked. Her voice meant business. They were called upon, one at a time, to approach the pan. Then she nudged each one in, showed them what the pan was for, with much pawing and smelling, then ordered them back into the line; they followed the orders like little soldiers. Her loud talking and their tiny meows of response throughout the lesson is what drew me to the scene.

I couldn't believe it. Each kitten behaved in character. Spoiled brat Blacky horsed around, whispered behind his mother's back, shot a few spitballs, but even he didn't dare leave the line. Missey, good little girl, daintily pattered up to the pan. Twinky, the runt, went scared, hesitant but brave. It was Patches who learned the lesson the quickest and best, she was so eager for the praise she never got. In a matter of minutes, four kittens had been toilet-trained. Willow looked up at me to have the feat acknowledged.

From then on, like a curtain coming down on their infancy, she withdrew herself from their needs, with an "I want my body back, you feed them, I'm finished." All except Blacky. She continued to nurse, wash, and dote on him in such an unfair manner, the other three gave her up in disgust. They bonded to us and our offerings of gruel, and behaved outrageously—curtain-climbing, furniture-tearing, hide-and-seeking—until Willow pleaded with us: "Get those hoodlums out of here or I'll go mad!"

Now we had to find adoptive parents—Freudian-oriented, of course—for all of them. Did we know four such pairs of parents? Fortunately, almost. We thought of keeping Blacky, he was so gorgeous and Willow was so attached to him; we probably should have, but my sister Elizabeth said she would love to have him. We were surprised. Elizabeth had never been a cat person. She

had invested an enormous love in only one
animal in the past—a delicate, blond, feath-
ery English setter named Lady who smiled,
and looked like Elizabeth—thin, fair, lean,
graceful. The dog was a mirror image of her
mistress. It was an arresting sight, the two of
them walking down a street together, Elizabeth's shoulder-length hair and Lady's setter
ears swinging in the wind.

Elizabeth was always one for perfection
and Blacky was that, a gleaming, Egyptian,
ebony cat rippling with male beauty. If she
wanted him, she should have him.

We grew up with my father's addiction to
Boston terriers, generations of them laden
with pedigrees and all named Chummy.
Nervous, hyperactive, overbred little creatures, they went into canine hysteria at the
slightest unexpected movement or noise.
Yankee dogs. They made life a hell for me. I
was a little girl as nervous, unreliable, and
high-spirited as the dogs. I jumped, I
twirled. They jumped, they twirled. Talk
about Olympic-quality ice skaters, our
Chummys could do *triple* axle jumps just
saying hello. My childhood was laced with

nips and bites about the ankles and thighs. I think I was testing Papa to see whom he loved more, whom he would banish first, them or me. It was always *me.* "Go to your room; you're upsetting Chummy."

But one glorious incident brought an end to the Chummys. I had just been given a new squirrel coat, my first fur. I think I was seven. I put it on, showed it off, twirled about, while the current Chummy, his tongue hanging out, breathed hard and wondered what squirrels were doing in the living room. Chomp. The bite on the thigh, right through the squirrel coat, sent me to the hospital. That ended the reign of Chummy forever.

Papa was sad and it was my fault. He missed worrying and fussing over those mad little dogs always creating a crisis, running off to neighbors, eating salami out of their garbage, slinking home vomiting, close to death, having to be nursed back to health so carefully. One slice of salami could kill a Boston terrier. Papa, the doctor, found that very challenging. He probably should have worried more about my nervous and digestive systems than theirs.

We were all nervous, moody, difficult, unpredictable terriers, the dogs, my father, and I. Which is probably what drew him to them and me. He made no bones about my being his favorite little girl—that didn't make Elizabeth very happy, but she was much preferred by Mama, which made it *almost* even, *then*. I didn't know Papa was mine, I didn't know much of anything, until much later when he had cause to worry about me a lot, as well he should have. I presented him with a classically tumultuous adolescence that made the antics of terriers seem like the suspended calm of heavy whipped cream.

Willow had no separation pangs when her kittens left one by one, except for Blacky. She refused to eat, and slept for a whole day when Blacky went to live with Elizabeth and Peter. And someone else I haven't thought of for years. How could I forget? Their parakeet, Tweetie!

Elizabeth had married a childhood sweetheart and became divorced five or so years later. She married a second time and that hadn't a happy ending either, except for the birth of my nephew, Peter. How we doted on him. The first grandchild is always the miracle of creation, and so it was even for Papa, the taciturn, cerebral patriarch. A boy! It wasn't *enlightened* to favor one sex over the other; after all, Papa was an early antisexist and anti-Fascist, wasn't he? And Mama—a feminist, in theory at least—had trained him. But still, a boy! after the trials of two girls.

Peter livened the house, shook up the petitpoint chairs and shot sun into the cool parlor.

Papa knew nothing of boys, except for Robert, my stepbrother, who was already half grown when Papa married Diana a year after Mama died. What a mess of porridge she brought and inherited when she joined forces with my father to conquer their separate lonelinesses. Diana had lost a husband, Papa had lost Mama. Diana brought Papa a growing boy and her own grief hardly faded. Papa gave her an adolescent, angry daughter (me); and Elizabeth, who was about to get married and needed a wedding planned; plus a restrained house filled with Mama's antiques as well as her not-laid ghost.

Robert needed a father, even an irascible,

complicated one, and he became as attached to Papa as Elizabeth and I were, even if Papa never threw him a ball and scoffed at that opiate for the poor: baseball. Years later, when Robert married and began to present Papa and Diana with *many* grandchildren before he and his wife, Harriet, were done, little creatures underfoot had become the norm. But Elizabeth's Peter was the first, a happy phenomenon in a sad house.

It has been said, "It is the bars of our cage or aviary which vanish away the moment we begin to sing."

Peter's father, a gifted painter and designer, had been fated to love both Elizabeth and Peter, but his need to twist and hurt overwhelmed him; he couldn't make the bars of his cage vanish.

It was not a singing time for Elizabeth, those years after her second divorce, which had been nasty and filled with recrimination, and left her pale, worn out, and deeply injured. Peter spent many summers with Papa and Diana, who was as loving a grandmother to him as if he were her own. When "Petie" was there, he brought them sun and

singing. Love was in the air. Peter's birth
had also made me an aunt, the next female
in line to protect him in the den—as wolves
in their wilderness wisdom know so well.

The summer Peter was seven and spending the summer in Peabody, I was also there
for a time, with Chucky, who was three, to
make it more fun and help out Grammy.
Elizabeth was away choreographing a revival of Moss Hart and Kurt Weill's musical
Lady in the Dark, with Hart directing, and
starring his wife, Kitty Carlisle. Elizabeth
would have a fascinating, hardwork time,
and hopefully some fun; she deserved it.
Later she said that all she could remember
was the odor of Moss Hart sweating in abject fear, he was so nervous, but it had gone
well.

Peter and Chucky were playing the game
of Dizzy in the Peabody parlor: How long
can you go in circles before you lose your
balance and fall down dead? Suddenly a
scream. Peter had circled himself against a
sharp corner of a stolid, indifferent antique
chest that wouldn't get out of his way, and
there was an ugly gash on his forehead. Off
to the hospital!

It was a gash that required many stitches.
"Mummy! Mummy!" Mummy wasn't there,
only an aunt. Papa was so upset, he kept
pacing in and out of the operating room,
overcome by the Shoemaker's Child Syndrome. I promised Peter anything if he
would allow the surgeon standing over him
with a syringe to inject his forehead with an
anesthetic and begin the stitching.

"What would you like most in the world,
Petie?"

"A horse."

"Oh, no, you can't have a horse in a city
apartment, darling."

"Then, a pony."

Serious negotiation went on: a cow, a calf,
a rabbit . . .

"How about a beautiful bird, a canary?" I
offered hysterically, looking at the gash right
over his eye. I didn't dare offer a dog or a cat
without Elizabeth's permission.

"A canary," Peter whimpered, and gave
in, but it took "a fat nurse sat on me!" an
aunt holding his hand on one side, and Papa
on the other to get the wound stitched up.

A bird it was, but not a canary. An eccentric, nonstop-talking parakeet named Twee-

tie went back to New York with Peter and lived long after he went off to college. Ancient Tweetie even survived the coming and going of Blacky, Willow's only son.

Tweetie taunted Blacky so, made him so crazed trying to figure out the mystery of her cage, why she was in and he was out, or vice versa, that Elizabeth finally had to find another home for the cat.

Blacky ended up living on a country estate and gracing it with his flawless, ebony beauty, but his new owner complained that he spent most of his time outside, sitting on the limb of a tree, on the watch for birds, except in the dead of winter. Queer for birds he was, we were told. His coat grew thick and luxurious because he was outside so much, but when he chose to come inside and lie on the hearth, he was something to behold. "We don't interest him at all," Blacky's new owner complained. "We're just pleased he likes the cuisine and deigns to honor our restaurant every night."

Blacky's life ended dramatically. When he was sitting way up high in his tree one day, he was so absorbed in trying to get a fix on a bird, he lost his reason and balance, came tumbling down, couldn't land on all fours, broke his neck, and died.

Blacky's leaving our apartment had ended the first chapter of our life with Willow. Wham, bang, she had brought us *births*— like the flowers that inevitably spring up over graves amidst the trees, climbing on the vagrant sunlight. Weeds, flowers, kittens, babies, all mewling and insisting . . . all to deny the dark from causing permanent damage.

The bewitching, wacky, wonderful process of birth and growth in our apartment, brought by Willow from the Ukrainian-Polish cellar, pregnant at the age of six months, her ensuing children . . . had helped to settle the ashes of a mad dog, the death of Willow I, and the rape and murder of my Aunt Edys.

Make Myself Known

What a way to begin. Did They think I didn't know my destined purpose? Of course I did. And didn't I come through this Time around, in the presence chosen for me? I certainly did.

Being an advancing spirit enclosed in the form of a cat is a curse, believe me. It might be I am to discover otherwise, in the advancements or retreats, and might one day find that being Cat is the pinnacle of peace. But at this moment I must make myself known within the strictures of Cat:

Be demanding. Insist your milk must be heated in that little yellow pot, the one they used after they rescued me. No cold milk! Refuse water completely. Create idiosyncrasies, phobias, character necessities. Reject food unless it's kidney or liver cooked just the tiniest bit, with a pinch of salt, a touch of onion. Take your place on her side of the bed at night; females must stick together. And don't move an inch from the crook of her arm, except in unusual circumstances when *tohobohu* (total disorder, confusion is what that means; I know some Hebrew from other Times) takes over the bed. In other words, lovemaking in their way.

With the first light of day, get up and bang the blinds to wake them. Make them stagger from their sleep, to put the little yellow pot on the stove for my warm milk. I cannot begin the day without it. If the banging on the blinds doesn't wake them, go into the living room, nibble on a plant, go back to the bedroom, and gag on the white Moroccan rug; *that* will make them jump up fast.

All of the above is hardly befitting a superior spirit, but what could one do, confined as one was in the body of a cat?

We soon discovered that Willow was a born neurasthenic with all the trappings: a tendency toward delicate digestion, frequent colds, allergies, shyness, aloofness, depressions brought on by the slightest whiff of rejection. Hers was a shaky nature in need of order. Yet despite all threatenings to faint and fold, there was a quick wit and ironic gaiety underneath, and, as in most classic cases of neurasthenia, the hidden structure of a survivor. They worry you to distraction and then outlive you.

In no time at all, the birth and nurturing of four notwithstanding, Willow emerged in front of our eyes a virgin queen born to rule, a female fashioned of steel, with an unrelenting will and curious beauty. But to throw you off guard, she would often play a little of Blanche DuBois.

The boy, Chucky, amused and annoyed her. He was, after all, her competitor-sibling when she was young. She dubbed Jules her adjudicator and protector; me, she made her bosom companion with whom she could be duenna, virago, pampered child, or critic.

Willow didn't like to be touched unless she asked for it. We finally figured out: One didn't hug a presence, it was undignified to be picked up like a toy, a kiss was an invasion of privacy, one didn't slobber over royalty. It was for royalty to bestow and the commoner to receive gratefully if royalty *chose* to bestow. Such were her rules, and we obeyed. Sometimes she honored Jules by sitting on his lap, with a paw set lightly on each of his knees, looking like a miniature lioness with a slight smile. What an honor; Jules would beam. What have I done to deserve this royal favor?

She chose to sleep with me at night, in the crook of my arm, all barriers down—it was the time for members of the secret order of Woman to be together, odors mingling, the comfort of like nestling against like. With me, she gossiped, confessed, advised, encouraged, spoofed, mimicked, competed, and listened. What a gift to have the perfect listener . . . as well as an editor-in-residence, I was soon to discover.

Settling In

Looking back, I figure I was here again to learn a life of words and reading minds, and I couldn't have found a better place, but let me be correct: I didn't find, I was found, according to the plan of the Absolute Peaceful Hand.

Two writers and a boy, in a city apartment filled with Oriental rugs, a grand piano; books, books, books. And all they did was talk, or so it seemed in the beginning.

The A.P.H. knew what It was doing, but I had no idea; I was too young. I knew, however, that I had a purpose. What it

was, I didn't know, but it propelled me to
learn as fast and best I could—always with
a little fear, always with questions, always
with surprise. I don't like surprises, even if
the nervous system of a cat is geared for
just that. Cock the ears, bush out the tail,
extend the whiskers to quivering. I hated
doing all of that, but I accommodated
myself to the tools I had, even the arching
of the back. I stopped at the growl; it was
beneath me. I never used my growl, but for
a few times and for extraordinarily good
reason.

It took me half a year to get used to the
apartment, stake out my own private
places, and get my wits together after my
kittens left.

I would have liked Blacky to stay, but it
wasn't worth the howl. Something in me
knew I wasn't made to be maternal
indefinitely, like Her.

Ground rules, dear reader: Those two
who found and saved me? I shall refer to
them as He and She; Him or Her, or They.
I choose to honor the humans by
capitalizing their pronouns *sometimes.*

There is something you must understand

about me. I have spent most of my life
thinking. If the Absolute Peaceful Hand
had wanted it otherwise, I would have been
a country cat. My days would have been
spent running through woods, climbing
trees, sniffing bushes, peeking down holes
in the ground, catching mice and birds,
running through tall grass. *There would
have been little time to think.* Which is why
It destined me to be where I am, in a city
apartment, with words and notes and
books and newspapers, with Him who
expounds by the hour about the ways of
the world, justice and conscience, and Her
who pounded the piano for hours in the
early days and dreamed out loud about
truth, beauty, balance.

So I warn you, I am a philosopher,
which is not exactly unexciting to my
mind, since it is like being a detective
stalking around in the dark, with a brain
for a flashlight, trying to discover what the
Absolute Peaceful Hand had in mind to
begin and end with.

They and the boy. The whole place was
geared to what the boy needed. Such
attention, fussing about the boy. Was he

happy? Was he sad? Was he learning, and
was what he was learning good enough?
Even elephants don't take that much time
to make their young independent.

Most animal childhood is short, just a
summer to learn! Then the cold rain turns
to snow and suddenly! there is survival.
Make it or die.

But my job was to observe and note, in
case the next Time around I might be
elevated or demoted to human.

Just when I was getting used to the
apartment, choosing places for thinking—a
drawer filled with linens, a blue velvet
pillow on a window seat overlooking the
park; and my favorite public place, a
Victorian lady's chair that I especially
liked, with its sweeping back and curved
arms perfect for curling into and serious
napping . . .

Just when I was getting used to her
playing the piano all day and trying to
understand what "composing" meant . . .
(It meant repeating the same thing over
and over, resting her head on the piano,
being nasty to me if I walked on the top of
the piano to touch her nose and see what

was wrong—she would push me away or
grab me and hug me, as if we were both in
some imminent danger. She and I were
alone a lot. He went to an office to
"produce" or "direct" when he wasn't
home pounding the typewriter. The boy
went off to school—as if they weren't
teaching him enough where he was.)

Just when I was getting used to those
crashing chords of hers, the songs she used
to sing as if her heart would break, or
others that had a hoppy, sunny feeling I
began to like and sing to myself . . .

Even if I didn't want to, I had to pay
attention to her. She would suddenly stop
what she was doing, the same phrase, over
and over, and ask me, "Willow, how does
that sound? Is it good?" She knew she was
good; people came and told her so, people
who knew about such things. I heard them,
picked up the vibrations in the air while I
made believe I was sleeping in the lady's
chair. Why did she need me to tell her she
was good?

The people who came only heard what
she finished. I had to hear what she was
making! If I didn't like it, I would leave

the room. If I did like it, I would jump
onto the piano, lie down, and purr. It
made her happy when I did that, lay there
while she "composed." She would say,
"Thank you, I like you there, this is a
lonely job, pussycat." That's what she did
when she didn't say "Go away!"

I learned fast that living with "artists"
and their moods was not easy, hers
especially. She was always a little off-
center, into herself, until the middle of the
day. He was the opposite. You could count
on his good humor, even at dawn for an
early breakfast. He and I are both alike in
that respect. If you can't greet the day in a
good mood, what's the point in being or
day? I *do* like my breakfast!

But I didn't like his scooping me up in
his arms as if I were a toy. I allowed it for
a second or two, because I didn't want to
hurt his feelings. He was the one to be
trusted for the important early-morning
things like food and a clean pan.

Just when I was getting used to it all,
suddenly they're packing! The boy left first,
to what they called "camp."

A few days later, a car was waiting

outside. She was yelling orders. He was carrying suitcases and books, even her music off the piano, and muttering, "It's as if we're moving away for good. Is all this necessary?"

And finally, out came a box for me, with a window on top. I began to tremble violently. It's back to the cellar! Why did they think I needed a window to see my way back to the cellar? I couldn't understand it. We couldn't all be going back to the cellar, could we?

And I had begun to trust them.

Suddenly they're trying to put me into the box, without a word to prepare me, to let me know what was happening. They had to stuff me into that box because I fought, screaming, "No! No! Not back to the cellar!"

In those days I was young and dumb in my ability to perceive, new at the game of words and reading minds, and They were just as dumb about how to communicate with me. They could have saved me the fear and trembling. I would have understood, if not in words, just by tone, the gentle confiding, if They had told me:

"Willow, we're *all* going away for the summer. We do this every year."

It took me the whole trip to get over the fear and trembling. My box was soaked in sweat and covered with my hair, which fell out as if I had been hit by a plague. Then, when we boarded a boat and I heard the roar of the engines and the slapping of the waves, I just closed my eyes and pleaded with small meows, over and over, for the Absolute Peaceful Hand to rethink my plight and take me back. Even if it meant to start over again in a cellar!

I refused to open my eyes until all motion had stopped, even when we left the boat and He was pulling a cart filled with suitcases as She held my box, peering in, trying to talk to me, guilty and too late as far as I was concerned. I refused to open my eyes when she said, "We're here, Willow, we're here! Smell the sea air!"

I refused to open my eyes until my box was put on something solid, a couch on a porch. I didn't know what a porch was at the time. I was so weak I had to be lifted out of the box, and only then did I open my eyes. I looked through the screens and

saw the water we had just escaped from—
the bay with a sunset in it. I took a deep
breath. The air was so strong it made me
sneeze.

And then I heard a mourning dove for
the first time.

What had happened was: We had come
to a place called Fire Island. And thereby
hangs a tale as well as part of my tail.

FIRE ISLAND

The Healing View

THE Long Island Indians knew very well the quarter-mile-wide, seventy-five-mile-long island in the Great South Bay. Beyond it, the wide ocean with its bluefish, bass, and tuna. Before it, the sparkling bay, a fisherman's dream stuffed with clambeds, crabs, eels. Food appeared by the millions, like shining torrents of rain, come spring and summer. It was their vacation spot long before the white man's boats came. The Indian cherished the thin strip of land because it was also a sentinel, a bulwark against the anger of the northeast winds that could eat away the mainland if the island were not there to ward

off the first blows. Indian mothers didn't
have to be watchful of the children here, for
there were no bears or wolves, nothing to be
cautious about except the three-leafed plant
growing everywhere that turned a fiery red
in late summer and caused *the itch*—if you
were foolish enough to touch it. The poison
ivy grew everywhere, between the scrub
pine, blueberry bushes, and beach plums. No
matter. Every gift of the Great Father had its
test large or small; every paradise had its entrance fee. The glorious fishing, the proud
white strands of sandy beach made up for
the penalty of the itch.

It was just a morning's canoe trip across
the peaceful bay that hid the delectable
clams to be baked or boiled over roaring fires
on the oceanside, as the sun sank and the
stars came, with song in the air and the children running free as the little sand crabs, the
seabirds at the water's edge.

There are stories about how the island got
its name. One was that the Indians made
bonfires on the oceanside to guide their deep-
sea fishermen safely home. Another: Either
white or red men made great fires to lure
cargo ships into thinking the island was the

mainland. Then the ships would founder on the banks and be easy prey for boarding and pirating. And in the not-so-long-ago, during Prohibition, rum-runners used the island as a base. Fast-motored, sturdy boats would sneak into the mainland coves in the dead of night, filled to the gills with illegal "firewater" that had been brought up or down the coast in the holds of oceangoing ships, then transferred to the smaller boats, which could maneuver the tricky inlets between the ocean and the bay.

When we began to spend our summers on Fire Island in the late 1950s, a few of those rum-running boats were still making the run, but now for people, not whiskey. The captain-owner of the fleet, a veteran of those wild and woolly days, was now old and legitimate but still had the look of a wily pirate who had seen and done everything to be imagined with a boat on a stormy sea. I always felt safe when he was at the wheel on bad-weather crossings, when the benign Great South Bay could whip itself up like a typhoon in the China seas. "No storm or police boat could ever beat this girl," he'd say, patting his wheel. "There ain't no secret she

or I don't know about this damn water under us."

The first time Willow crossed the bay (in
fear and trembling, with her eyes shut tight),
it was to be our seventh summer on the island, and we were on one of the captain's
new, sleek, two-decker boats. He had become very successful plying the people trade;
there was no way to get over to the community we were heading for unless the captain's
fleet ferried you across, plus everything the
one store needed to feed you.

It was a luxury to spend summers on Fire
Island, but somehow we always managed it
on a free-lance income that varied dizzily,
yet always righted itself in time to rent a
summer house, pay for private schools, even
a housekeeper—a necessity our first summer.
That first summer I had needed all the support and protection possible, and Jules saw
to it that I got it. I needed to make believe I
had not cracked wide open in a nervous
breakdown. How to keep a little boy's life
normal in the face of that? A summer in a
big, old, salt-weathered house overlooking
the bay, for his mother; ocean walks, a place
for the inner and outer eye to take in that

one-hundred-eighty-degree healing view of
the universe.

Never to have nearly, never to have not,
never to have nearly not died is never to
have lived, really. In retrospect, how lucky I
was to be able to afford the five-days-a-week
Freudian analysis, with its opening of the
sluice gates, frightening as it was—the
churning, debris-laden water breaking loose
and the dam itself giving way to allow the
past to catapult out at terrifying speed, in
slow motion. In the confusion of private
chaos and regression that is breakdown
("Take care of me!"), I was like a hump-
backed whale with its migratory compass on
the blink. I had wandered under a bridge
and up a river, instead of down the coast
with the rest of the family. If there were no
samaritans to coax my lost and lumbering
being back into familiar, open water, I was
doomed.

How had it happened that I was drowning
in unanswerables, that I had lost my center,
and Anxiety, like a spider, had lured it into
its web? Anxiety has no time sense; it sways
in an unswept corner of a room, waiting for
victims, unless a determined broom finds it.

Why does a roller coaster that has made the run up and down a thousand times suddenly lose a bolt and plunge people to their death? Or the metal of an airplane part disintegrate from fatigue in midair? A combination of fate, human error, neglect, a dose of stupidity? The reasons usually are discovered with astoundingly brilliant analysis by the experts in such matters. Miles are combed for every tiny bit of metallic evidence of the crash.

In the breakdown of a human spirit, midair, it is the elusive chain of mythic connection and ritual that becomes frayed, the drama of the present and the past tearing apart *at the same moment,* and the shock of recognition too much to bear. Hurtling to the ground you go, or wheeling through the sky you fall—a puppet to the earth, limbs shredded like paper when character breaks open, explodes.

Breakdown. A physical dizziness takes over, a need to stop the clock in some remembered past time when the call "Mama! Papa! Comfort me in the dark!" could bring the footsteps running.

(Grown woman, ghosts cannot come running!)

Logic doesn't command the days of breakdown, so the only wish is to crawl on all fours, closer to the ground, an infant in a tantrum.

Logic does command repetitive dreams of being lost in dense forest, when, as in my case, the dreams were *true.*

The summer I was five, Mama, a trained nurse, had given her services to a children's camp called Camp Nitgedeigit (meaning "Don't worry" in Yiddish; subtext: Come the revolution!). The hilarious irony of the name will soon become clear. It was a Communist children's camp, and I, naturally, had to be there with Mama for the summer. Elizabeth was away at another camp, and Papa, the doctor, was at home taking care of the sick but came to see us on weekends.

During the day I was allowed to join the other children, but at night I had to sleep with Mama in the infirmary, which was her sleeping quarter as well. During the day I played games, learned to sing "The Internationale"—"Arise ye workers of starvation, arise ye workers of the world. . . ."

But at night Mama left me in our hut-infirmary deep in the woods and went off to discussion groups. Up the hill where the other children slept, the counselors on watch could hear my screams of fear that told of ogres, wild boars, tree branches turning into serpents in the moonlight. The counselors came running, but not Mama; she was too far away to hear me. When told of my cries, she was furious that her child-rearing plans had been intruded upon by counselors who took it upon themselves to carry me up the hill to spend the night in a cozy bunk filled with giggling or sleeping children. Mama, queen of charity bestowing her nursing graces on the commonality for the summer, laid down an edict: No one was to intervene in my behalf. I think she truly believed she was building character in her princess, and had a more secret thought she could never have admitted to: A little princess does not sleep with the commonality. So I screamed and never forgot those summer nights.

Until a time came for all such secrets of the past to tumble out like starved, hollow-eyed nymphs sealed up in a tree trunk, suddenly released by a bolt of lightning that had split the trunk in two. Out they rolled, eyes ablaze with anger and no forgiveness.

That same summer in Camp Don't Worry, I also almost drowned. (It's beginning to sound like one of Dick Gregory's laughter and tears comedy routines, in which he describes the dire poverty of his childhood: There was no father; his mother took in washing, and while the sheets were drying she hung them in the windows of their tenement and they had curtains for a few hours; they were always wondering where their next meal would come from; he and his brothers took turns going to school because there weren't enough clothes to go around . . . and *then* came the Depression!)

If it had not been for a counselor who brushed against something on the floor of the lake, put his face in the water to see what it was, picked me up by my hair, then my armpits, carried me to the beach where he gave me mouth-to-mouth resuscitation, then forced me to throw up the water in my lungs . . . I most definitely would have been *missing in action.* Mama had been there, sitting

on the sand, talking to someone. Maybe I
had wandered into deep water, away from
the beginner swimmers close to shore. I remember being pushed, there were so many
children in the water. The waterfront of that
idealistic camp was so badly run it's a wonder they didn't lose a child a week to the
glory of "the movement." I remember going
down, down, in bewilderment and defeat,
and a flickering picture of Mama's proud,
handsome head wound about with her thick,
shining braids—she was talking to someone
and I couldn't tell her what was happening,
she was too far away. And I remember the
look of guilt and horror on her face when I
lay on the sand after I had been *saved*.

(To this day, when I sit on a beach I cannot stop counting heads in the water,
whether they belong to me or not. I was
made an obsessive lifeguard for life.)

In a child's simple, trusting soul, when a
mother is not there in the dark or light, it
must be that she is lost or has died. Or
worse, the child is unworthy to be watched
over and loved. So reasons a child—*and* a
grown-up in breakdown.

That summer must have been etched in

my mind, like a cave painting preserved on its rock wall in the dark for aeons, as the definitive rendition of the child and the woman-to-be who broke years later. Unlike the cave paintings of ancient people that must be preserved in the dark, to protect their tales of life and death, it's a miraculous fortuity when cave paintings on the mind are stumbled upon, discovered, and the light and air allowed to destroy them, obliterate them into shadowy scratchings. Then it's hard to tell whether they were made by the nails of an animal or the soul of a human. Even so . . . as on rock, so on the mind, the indentations will always remain as evidence that a picture had been etched, a character formed, and its resonance, though far-off as a Martian flute, still to be dealt with: A picture had been drawn of a child longing for the safety of love.

In the 1950s it was *de rigueur* to be not "in therapy" but in "deep analysis"—the real thing. I was in deep analysis with my sister's analyst. What a mistake to start with, though I couldn't blame the woman for being curious about, wanting to tackle *the younger one,* the object of my sister's jealousy, rivalry, and death wishes. Had Elizabeth ever told her about the time Mama was bathing me in the tub, turned her back to rinse something in the sink, and Elizabeth was watching the baby have her bath? The baby in the large, Victorian tub went under, the Elizabeth stood there, transfixed by the bubbles, without saying a word. Until Mama turned around and screamed. Had Elizabeth told the analyst that she had been spanked for her silence?

Good lord, there had been a first almost-drowning, before the second! Does a seven-year-old know the difference between a rag doll or a naked baby floating on its face? Given the intensity of our competitiveness, it was my mistake, as well as the analyst's, for starting up with her in the first place. I needed *my own in everything,* after years of being compared with the elder, taken for her twin. I wasn't her twin. Elizabeth was white-skinned and green-eyed, with burnished hair and the lean body of a dancer, which she became, a breathtaking, lyrical one. I was taller, dark-haired, olive-complexioned; my knees were chubby, I sweated more, my breasts were fuller—I was a more vulgar edition of her refinements. But seen separately, we seemed like two halves of the same egg. My beloved enemy. How I admired her, was fearful of her disdain, tried to be like her and gave up. Instead I went my own uncharted course, in a Rube Goldberg–ish vehicle of such internal combustion complication, with an absurd amount of wheels and brakes . . . I often found myself traveling at breakneck speed standing still.

The analyst's second mistake was that she so resembled my mother, it was amazing. Her third mistake: She led me to the well, pushed my head in, and forced a crucial analytic scene: Drink of your mother. Why did you feel that she didn't love you? Did you fancy you were powerful enough to have killed her, been responsible for her death? Then at the end of the hour the Mama look-alike said, "I'm going to Europe for a few months. We'll continue this when I get back. If you can't manage, I'll give you the name of someone. . . ."

Betrayed. I reasoned like the child she had brought me back to, and knowing little of that child, I fell into nothingness. I didn't

deserve to trust anyone—even if I paid for it!
It was simply my lot to have had a mother
who died when I was fourteen and another
who abandoned me when I was thirty, both
without warning.

Years later, a colleague of the analyst and
a friend of ours offered the thought that I
had probably been the one serious mistake
my analyst had made in her career; she was
so respected, even renowned in the field. She
had studied in Vienna, with a student of
Freud or maybe even with Freud himself.
Cold comfort. Our friend shook his head in
sympathy. "The time to pull down the fences
is crucial, the crux of the art and science of
therapy." His eyes actually filled up.

Wait, wait . . . to be utterly fair, the patient comes to the analytic hour like a Pandora's box. Only a wizard with supernatural
powers can foretell its contents and mixtures
and what will happen when they rise up and
mix with air. When the past and the present
meet, and the stress on the metal makes it
give way . . .

A month or so before the analyst's an-
nouncement that she was leaving, and the
analysis had become intense, Chucky had a

severe nosebleed that couldn't be stemmed. His doctor came rushing through the streets of New York, not an easy or usual thing. When he arrived, there was blood all over the crib and the walls of the nursery. Two attempts on the doctor's part to stem the flow failed. Alarmed as I, he was about to drive us to a hospital, when the third attempt to pack the nose succeeded. Only when it was all over did I collapse and faint for the first time in my life. My shining little boy had almost betrayed me by almost bleeding to death. Dizziness: the symptom that heralded the breakdown and stayed for a year, off and on. I was dizzy with fear, present and past betrayal, ancient anger.

That same month, the husband of a dear friend proposed that we have an affair. Shocked, I reeled away from him, but the afternoon air simply heard my "Are you crazy?" . . . my fake-amused but carefully firm no. (Oh, I was in control of that lustful, longing moment that forgets everything, I thought.) Was he out of his mind? Four friendships would have been lost, betrayed!

A month after the analyst left for Europe, when roses were blooming in gardens somewhere and day lilies opening with languid pops in the July heat . . . I exploded mid-air, in a ball of flame.

Breakdown. A Swedish masseuse came every morning (doctor's orders), and for several hours she calmed the anarchy in my muscles and nerves that all seemed connected to the right lobe of my brain, where a searing pain would shoot out without warning, like a hammer's blow—to remind me that my unconscious, with its stored memory life, had turned into an enemy. Its shadow lurked in the dark passages of my day, its muscles pumped up and ready for the unexpected blow at any moment, demanding that I acknowledge its existence, its rights, in the only way left to it: a Zen blow to the head. "Here! Take that! *That* pain is real!"

And in the afternoons, a womb-taxi took me to an old and wise sachem, a strict Freudian analyst with half-closed cobra eyes. Protective but dispassionate, he led me to the inevitable battle-ground every day, played my second, handed me the weapon of my choice, and oversaw the daily duel with that pumped-up-muscled-enemy, whose leaping brilliance across voids, down triple flights of stairs to the heart in one stunning leap could render me stunned into silence, my weapon of defense or denial on any particular day, limp and ineffectual as a plucked stalk of wild grass.

The cobra-eyed one had much investigation to do. Miles had to be combed for every bit of evidence of the crash, and the reasons discovered with astoundingly brilliant analysis.

Slowly he led me to the well again, but didn't push my head into its depths; rather he sprinkled it like holy water on my ill forehead. After all, are not the past, memory, and dreams the most holy of experiences to learn from, not to drown in? Chew, eat the past like grapes, he urged. Swallow, digest, maybe even enjoy the meat; but spit out the pits!

Being *Mother* saved me. I knew that, even in the numbness of the breakdown. I had a four-year-old child who needed me to continue teaching him the secrets of loving, the wonder of being. For him, I wrote some of my most lyrical, happy-hopping-beat children's songs in that dark period: "Close your eyes, my little boy, and rest your head on my shoulder. The world will wait, the world will wait while you rest your head on my shoulder. . . ." "There's nothing to be upset about, everything has an in and out. . . ." "Look, look at the blue sky, white clouds floating by. My, what a lovely day today, let's clap hands and sing away. . . ." "And a bang-a, bang-a, bang-a, and a bang-a bang-boo! Oh, I haven't any money, but I wish you'd be my honey. . . ."

Love and light. There could never be enough of both, to sing about, what with the blackness that had been mine. I was determined not to pass it down to my shining little boy, as so often happens in so many families. One day you wake up and realize that you have done what was done to you, unwittingly, programmed by ancient reflexes. Not again for this child, to be overwhelmed by the haunts, the fears, the why-don't-you-love-me-different blues.

Chucky especially liked: "Let's go for a walk in the woods. Let's find a silvery stream to wade, a blueberry patch to pick. Let's hop on a ship to Borneo, let's fly on a plane to Japan! Let's climb up a mountain in India that's never been climbed by man! Then it's home for a walk in the woods, the woods, with your hand in mine." What a different woods than mine I tried to make it, and always with the *we* implicit in the "Let's go."

The little boy grew up to be an avid mountain climber, a prudent yet adventurous man, and rather fearless, I think. I must have succeeded in my mother part, in tandem with Jules, a loving, giving man.

Breakdown gives way to insight, and insight gives way to change. Insight comes slowly, like the careful stringing of pearls. A jewel, a knot, another jewel, another knot. It's an insanely difficult act to make a necklace in the midst of tempest, to sit quietly with trembling fingers, while the well water spills over from the sides of your eyes. But with insight also comes healing, the return of laughter, the possibility of joy.

Change. I question the idea: "The character of a man is his fate." It's the basis of the greatest tragedies and dramas, but who wants to be a leading character in a tragedy, veering into the inevitable without brakes, because you cannot change!

Brought up as I was, by those flawed, wonderful characters, my parents with their dreams of a socialist utopia, I cannot help but bring in the world. They did teach me that I was not an island unto myself. The grand, analytic process of change is still in its infancy, whether it concerns the democracy of a self longing to be free of rigidity, obsession, and anger, or the world of selves beyond one's private world. Democracy and its unwritten laws for change without anarchy is still a dream that takes your breath away. Illness of the soul is fascism. Only the mad can tolerate being the helpless victims of themselves.

Island: ". . . a refuge from the menacing assault of the sea of the unconscious. A place to regenerate the conscious will."

Sea. Ocean. "Where it all began . . . Both the positive and negative. The sun dies in the sea every evening and is reborn from its every dawn. Life and death. Chaos and serenity. Love. Mother."

The above are quotes from a Jungian dictionary. I bathe in its conjectures whenever I want to bathe in the meaning of words. In my changing years that continue to change,

my sense of it now is: Probably a vinaigrette
of the genius of Freud and Jung, mixed well,
is the best aromatic for the fainting heart.
It's the combination of *Know thyself* and *One
with All* that seems so crucially important in
these latter days of the twentieth century,
what with the species of Human, with its
fumes, foams, and poisons, hell-bent on denying that the slow killing of the All is the
suicide of Self.

     ૎   ૎

All of this I told to Willow, how we had
come to the island seven years ago, and why.
I told her on the boat, but she wasn't listening. She was too frightened by the throbbing
of the engines as we made our way across the
bay.

Sisters

IN THE late 1950s and early 1960s Fire Island had a swept-clean, silent feel, discreet clapboard cottages large and small, with their old wickered porches, all seasoned by the salt winds. The pervasive sounds were of waves breaking on the oceanside, the caw-caw calling of seabirds, cardinals and blue jays fighting for their territorial branches in the stunted pines, the plaints of mourning doves, the occasional wheels of a wagon being pulled "to market" by some friend. There were no strangers then. And the loudest noise was the setting sun plopping into the bay.

On the nights of a full moon, there might be running feet up the walks, and laughter on the way to the ocean to see the water turned silver. But you didn't mind the midnight hilarity, you were one of them, with sleeping children left behind in the cottages and no guilt about it. Children, somehow, knew they had to sleep like stones on such nights, when their young parents dared to leave them and skip up the walks to bay at the moon, dance down the dunes onto the beach for a well-earned caper of lunar madness.

Twenty-five years later it's wall-to-wall Westchester, suburbia. It started with a community tennis court. Bad news; a tennis club had to follow. As insidiously as the tennis club grew (its wack-wacks drowning out the birds), so suddenly there were sailboats everywhere, and worse, motorboats and seagoing yachts. A new breed had arrived, wearing summer chic—new denims designed to look like they'd seen twenty years before the mast, or a lifetime in a potato field, honorably faded from sweat and years of washboards. Or they'd be wearing hotpants whiffs of the Côte d'Azur, sullen glamor. Gleaming, oiled-down women, pudgy-faced executive types haircutted to perfection, even the bald ones, sail into the dock at the wheels of their new toys.

The *arrivés* arrive. They build their *House & Garden* cathedral-ceilinged, octagonal-windowed, mammoth-patioed hideaways that tower over the clapboard cottages. Whether Bach or rock, it doesn't matter if it murders the silence when it ricochets down the walks, booming out from state-of-the-art stereos.

You can't hear the setting sun anymore, what with the artful spenders invading at that very hour, in seaplanes and jam-packed ferries.

Can you imagine the need to build swimming pools on a quarter-mile-wide island, with an ocean on one side and a bay on the other? Ah, clever, the prescient rich with an eye to the day when ocean and bay will be polluted with the silence of death, but *they* will have their pools and hot tubs . . . while we others, only the memories of the swept-clean, silent beauty of other days.

* * *

In 1963, the little cottage, no more than fifteen feet away from the Great South Bay, was all we needed. It had been a fishermen's hut in the early days, a one-room haven to sit out a northeaster. Later it became two rooms, a kitchen and a bedroom, with a porch running the length of the cottage, an almost-living room where I placed an electric piano against the inside wall, away from the weather. Chuck and Peter were away at camp. Elizabeth had rented her own place a few walks away from the cottage. I think we were in a cooled-down state that summer, she and I, one of the sibling off-again times, but we always managed to be near one another, the love being stronger than the hate. At summer's end the kids were to join us in the cottage and sleep on the porch, rain or shine; they liked that plan. Jules would arrive on the "Daddy boat" every Friday, for the weekend. The cottage was a doll's house, the deck of a ship, a clapboard tent. During the week it was for Willow and me, and a summer of work. I was writing a musical called *Mrs. Godolfin Says "No."*

* * *

"We're going to have a wonderful summer" I said to Willow, placing her on one of the couches on the screened-in porch while trying to ignore her shaking little body. She was making hiccuping, grunting sounds deep in her stomach. I picked her up, touched her nose with mine, looked deep into her eyes, and transmitted what the island had meant to me when I needed it—a healing place. And just because it's new doesn't mean it has to be frightening, silly. . . .

"Look who's calling who silly! I can tell you right away, this place might be good for you, but it's not going to be good for me! We obviously don't share the same definition of *good.*"

She looked out at the expanse of sky and bay, still grunting her disapproval, then jumped out of my arms and slithered all around the cottage, seeing that it was small enough to manage, though the smells of old, sea-drenched wood were going to mean some getting used to. She found a closet that had a curtain for a door, walked in, and didn't come out for two days. Hunger fast. After that she flung the curtain aside with a paw, stood there for a moment to observe

the required stage entrance of a great trage-
dienne, and walked slowly to the couches on
the porch, where she had decided to make
the best of it, and where, she had to admit, it
was full of drama—people walking, on bicycles, the bay, sky, clouds, birds! the ever-
changing light, and dogs! . . . and listening
to me work at the electric piano.

I was determined to make her a normal
cat who loved to skitter out the door, take
long curious walks, discover the cool of un-
derbrush, everything that crawls, flashing
bird wings; then find her way home to slurp
up milk and eat ravenously, flop herself
down, fat with food and secret adventures.

How wrong could I be? Willow didn't
slurp, she sipped. She never ate ravenously,
she picked about the edges of her food in
concentric circles, always leaving a mound
in the center, which she never returned to
eat; that was for the servants. No finicky
duchess could make believe she didn't need
food for existence better than Willow could
—with her lightly sautéed chicken livers and
her milk warmed in her little yellow pot.

She was a scrimshaw cat etched in bone, a
cameo cat, a found moment of beauty, like

coming upon an exotic type of butterfly with
outstretched wings, sitting on a bush, or a
sudden view of a green alfalfa meadow, or a
phrase of music that hits your heart and you
don't mind the sudden death at all.

And I wanted to make her casual, independent, out, out you go now, into the
world, scramble in the sand, roll in the sun?
Not on your life! she said the first time I put
her down in the sand and high grass in front
of the cottage. She would have none of it and
fled back to the cottage door, waiting for me
to open it, with murder in her eyes. "You
still don't know who I am, do you!?"

Once in the house, her fastidious self went
crazy with the sand in her paws. She washed
and washed and gagged on the fine grains,
and the look on her face was: You mean, you
would like me to walk out there in that gar-
gantuan litter pan? You must be mad.

The first thing we always did after unpacking was to walk to the ocean for that
long look of the city-wounded, a gulp of the
universe over water, a deep breath of freedom. When we got back, there she was, her
little face with its white cross on the forehead, anxiously peering out from behind the

screened porch. We were humming and skip-
ping and she veered away from us, not being
familiar with such barefoot antics. But when
the chicken livers appeared, as they did in
the city, and the little yellow pot on the
stove, she realized that all was as it should
be, at least for now.

It was on the porch couches that she spent
her first week, listening to me work, watching me go and come from *out there,* the sun-
sand-water thing that kept me in an unusual
good mood, even at the piano. She observed
me with a weighty patience, in the meantime
making every inch of the little cottage her
own, and the attitude of her delicate body
saying: Don't worry about me, I'll be fine;
what is meted out I will accept with grace.
Her studied casualness was a lie, for her nose
never stopped twitching, picking up the sea-
pine-fish smells. Excited she was, and trying
to hide it, just delaying the day when *she*
would decide to venture out of her own free
will, all the way to the steps outside the
kitchen door.

In many ways Willow resembled my sister
Elizabeth.

All composure, studied thought, Elizabeth

had not an unironed moment in her life that
was obvious. She sniffed the ordinary, the
quick shot, the vulgar, and turned her back,
as if even the act of observing them had
made her guilty of gross indiscretion, a betrayer of the Absolute Ideal. It was our
mother who had pressed that into her first
daughter's being, as well as the Socratic notion that the rule of the aristocrat of spirit
and intellect, the privileged one who *knows,*
must govern and prevail over the undis-
ciplined, mentally unkempt, ignorant and
unruly. I was the latter, a foot-stomping, bi-
cycle-riding, catch-as-catch-can, rebellious
improviser, a swinging-through-the-trees little girl who just happened to find herself living in a house in which control, intellectual
pursuits, reining in the spirit by rule and
study was the road to Oz. Of course, it
rubbed off on me, made its imprint—that
search for balance, harmony, reason. But I
made believe it didn't, for years.

While I played mumblety-peg and jacks,
always with dirt under my nails, Elizabeth,
the perfect substitute to realize our mother's
own unfulfilled ambitions, was beginning her
regimented life—grueling dance classes, col-

lege, the study of philosophy at Harvard with the illustrious Professor Alfred North Whitehead.

While I was always absent without leave.

Ingrained in Elizabeth's lyrical body (she was born only to be a dancer, with her small-breasted, long, attenuated torso, her tiny waist, racehorse legs, the bones in her feet, the weight of her muscles all made to fly in and sculpt the air) was her vision and demand that every moment of life be choreographed, whether sitting in a chair, cooking, dressing, coiffing her hair, or making a dance. That impossible demand of herself was like the moment of perfection in a ballet *pas de deux,* when the ballerina on toe, with neck arched, arms extended like willow branches, one leg extended in a gravity-defying reach, stands posed, leaning gently against her partner; while music, the most perfect of the arts, sustains them as if it were solid as a bridge. Every waking moment of her life, even when she was dying, Elizabeth wrestled with what denied her that perfection.

Even with the tubes of a respirator threaded into her nose, down her throat, her

eyes wild with questioning but not wanting
an answer to the question since the question
was: Am I dying? Is this it? This way? The
obscenity of medical technology was astride
her like a slobbering monster and about to
break her mind. But even so, her white brow
with its moist, fine skin had frowned in tuto-
rial disapproval; her hands gestured a dansi-
cal no, no, no!, this form has no meaning, it
must be stopped, I will not tolerate it!

We made it possible that her sense of grace
not be offended *for a day more* by those who
had no idea whose mind and body lay in that
white-lit, high-tech bed of pain.

Though the wise ones insist: To accept
death as part of life is to lose one's fear, embrace a stoical peace, earn a card-carrying
membership in the Eternal Order of things;
for me, it was not peaceful or promisingly
eternal for my "big sister" to die, for the belt
of jealousy, emulation, and love that bound
us to be cut. The sibling placenta that had
fed us for a lifetime was being severed by
deepening doses of morphine. Slowly, slowly
she slipped back into the fathomless sea, taking with her the emotional noise of a lifetime
that belonged *only* to us, defined us, our own

special music . . . now to become thin ech-
oes, fainter and fainter. And I? To become
someone different—the survivor, older,
amazed by the breath of mortality on the
back of my neck, or a frontal, sneaky blow to
my ribs every once in a while, to remind me
I had experienced the absolute knowledge of
my own death through hers. Until Elizabeth
died I was the "little sister," gluttonous
owner of a Present Time that would go on
forever.

After her death there was to be an unholy
rankling, the bumping sound of black, an
unease. At other times, a curious physical
phenomenon: the sensation of a theme
caught in the corner of my eye, in a blink
shuttered away too fast to catch. A repetitive
exercise of an open eye clutching and losing,
clutching her *look remembered,* as if it were
a banister. It deceives me that it's grounded,
solid-set in stairs; it crumbles in my hand,
yet holding on, I climb and fall and climb, as
I remember.

I have a portrait of two women in the corner of my eye. We rise together on the stairs
—two apparitions through a fire, through
her spirit trailing smoke; through our fumes

of jealousy and love. Two sisters *always,* bound at the waist by a glistening wire. She, the elder, first, *even* in death; I, the younger, after . . . following in her wake of family pain and laughter. There she is, at the top of the stairs, serene. But I? I gasp for breath in the smoky mourning air, as if she had died today, yet I *know* it was I who threw her ashes to the sea. They fell light as feathers, bony pink, to join the rolling sand and shell, and a school of minnows looked surprised and bit. I know . . . I saw it!

Elizabeth is now all dream and beautiful in the blinking, shuttering away-too-fast-to-catch. I am real. How she must envy me for that. She need not envy me. It was I who gave her to the sea.

The Tale of a Tail

It was the turning point in my life as a cat, that first summer of mine on Fire Island. In my life not as a cat, but *their* cat. Being a domestic animal, your fate is not entirely of your own making. Being in a state of benign slavery, loving despotism, is more to the point. That is, when the situation is good and you're not a ninny and don't bite the hand that feeds you. When the situation is bad, then it's a prison sentence, torture, maybe even murder. From the stories I have heard about unfortunate human children and other animals, they're caught in a trap from the minute they are born or adopted.

So you see, being *theirs,* I *had* to accompany them to Fire Island. I *had* to look forward to nothing but sitting on a porch and staring out a screen—my decision that was, being who I am; I detested the sand!

I have waited a long time to write this particular episode of my life, because how do you know what an episode means unless you've lived a long time past it and can look back with some learning under your ribs? I'm beginning to wonder how long I will live. That thought doesn't really bother me, because I know from experience there is no forever for anything with a heartbeat or a root. Come to think of it, I'm not sure I'd like to be a tree that's lived for two hundred years. It must be boring to have to watch so many repetitions, generations of children fighting over a game of ball under my shade, then those generations of children growing up and fighting not for a ball but what they call an idea worth killing for. This human idea about killing for an idea is something I have to think about for a long time yet. For animals with superior brains, killing someone else can mean dying yourself, and there goes your precious brain in your small forever, down the drain. And who cares? You're just a victim of an idea. The thing is to avoid being just a number, even if it's only in your own deep self.

As cats come and go, I think I succeeded very well in that department. Ideas come and go, everything comes and goes. It's how you come, not go, that interests the Absolute Peaceful Hand. I know that many times over. And another thing I know: It leaves you alone a lot, to test your truth. It's not peaches and cream, that demanding Hand, as I am about to recollect.

After two weeks in that little cottage, I was going out of my mind and trying my best to show it. The twanging of the electric piano was driving me mad, not like the Steinway She worked on at home. Home. How I missed the window seat looking down at the park, my lady's chair. So I meowed every time she worked on that instrument of torture to my ears.

Things were not going well between us.
She would command me to be quiet in a
most uncivilized twanging voice of her
own, whereupon I would take myself off,
into that closet with nothing but a curtain
for a door, lick my fur down, cover my
ears, and make believe I wasn't where I
was.

Victim, I would mutter to myself, victim.
This life of mine is nothing but learning
how to be a victim. And I would victimize
myself to sleep with the hum of the
injustice of it all. How long did she think I
could listen to her songs from *Mrs.
Godolfin Says "No"* without anywhere to
escape to?

So I ventured out to the steps of the
kitchen porch at the side of the house. So I
went down one step. So I went down one
step more. And I sat. The twanging was
muffled but easier to bear outside, but it
was comforting to hear her voice inside,
singing, "It's so lovely to live on a street/
where you know everybody you
meet. . . ."

Why not? Why not take a little walk?
Carefully, I made my way down the bay

walk. There was sea grass on either side. I had never walked in grass. Suddenly I was overtaken with a desire to run! I plunged into the grass, into the thin, waving lines that parted as I ran. What fun making them move. I skittered from side to side, feeling the whoosh of the green lines. I ran and ran, into the grass, out of the grass, and all of a sudden I found myself way up high on a wooden platform, with a tremendous sound of thudding and gurgling and crashing coming close, going away. The sound went from my paws all through my body. There it was—the ocean! So that's where she went every day and came back sweeter and beaming.

I sat on the platform, curled my tail under me, and looked. From way up high, which is where I like to look from, I saw that there was nothing to be afraid of, though it was awesome indeed—all that water moving up and back like a restless spirit, but not unhappy. To the contrary, it was full of itself, it was perfect in itself, a whole that needed nothing to make itself but itself!—a state I knew to be the true way of being. I was not afraid.

I must do this every day, I said to
myself and turned about on the platform to
find my way back to the cottage with Her
in it, my home and safety for the time
being. I had never used my homing instinct
before, and I remember standing there for
a thinking moment, a little confused. I
know *now* I could have found my way,
except . . .

He sprang out of nowhere! A black-and-
white cat. He blocked my way, sat right
down in front of me, and grinned. The first
example of my species that I had been
close to since my days in the cellar, but I
was not quite afraid. I had, after all, grown
to my full size, true, smaller and more
delicate than most, yet this creature, twice
as large, did not frighten me; probably
because he was grinning and I didn't smell
anger, though I should have smelled other
things.

So I sidestepped him and tried to
proceed. So he sidestepped me. I did the
same. Silly grin. Foolish. He was quick as
an arrow, though, and suddenly was at my
rear, sniffing without a by-your-leave. I let
out a yowl of annoyance, which he must

not have expected, for he jumped back into the grass and let me continue down the path. Jump! He was beside me, walking with me, turning his head to look at me, and with that silly grin. I ran. He ran. I fled into the grass. So did he, after me. I raced out into the path. So did he, nuzzling, laughing. . . .

I had played games with the boy, mostly to please him and watch his amazement over my ability to catch a ridiculous little ball, but all at once it dawned on me that one of my own kind was trying to play with me. Cat's play!

My nature was not to be intrigued by a game of hide-and-seek, but suddenly I was being captured by something. I knew it was a laugh, though I had never laughed before. I could feel it growing inside me like a bubble, a lightness, a freedom burst out! . . . I took off through the grasses and dared him to find me! Crisscross through empty places, around houses, this way, that way, like lightning I was gone, like lightning he appeared. Delightful games.

And I could feel something else

happening, some warm, some feel, some smell; some energy right from the Hand of the Absolute drove us under the dark, wet pilings of a strange house far off somewhere, far off from everything. The cottage with Her in it was a dream. The Absolute was commanding me to do what I was supposed to do in the body of a cat, and I gave myself to it, yowling at first, in surprise. Then I became dumb to All. Then . . . screamed in pain beyond pain. He had bitten the end of my tail half off, in a paroxysm of ecstasy! and disappeared as fast as he had appeared in front of me before the game began.

There I was, leaning against the wet pilings of a strange nowhere, covered with mud, blood mixed with mud at the end of my tail, utterly alone, limp with pain, lost. I had just been loved in the way of cats. I had given myself willingly and as commanded. Something told me to lick the blood. Lick, lick . . . I fell into darkness. I awoke in the middle of the night, shivering and hot, my ears bursting with the sounds of the uncaring All, my faint cries nothing more nor less than a speck of the earth under me. I was nothing more nor less than the soundless grass, the booming of the huge water in the night. My pain, my lostness was nothing. Of no importance.

Yet, listen well to what happened: I could hear my heart and feel a fire in me that made me stand up when the light came. I slithered on my stomach, dragging my broken tail out from under the damp shadows, my clotted fur rubbing against everything that was busy crumbling, dying, awakening—crickets, dead spiders, ant eggs, roots like razors, the foul droppings of large and small. . . . I slithered away from the sound of the ocean toward the quiet hum of the bay. The fire in me told me *that* like a quivering needle, it was the strangest feeling. A quivering needle was pulling my poor body through masses of air, pebbles, stones that cut like knives, even the bending grass felt like knives, and flies flitted around my bloody tail. All not caring whether I was or whether I wasn't. I was of no matter . . . except for the fire that fed the needle that led me to the back steps of the cottage.

I dragged myself up the stairs and

collapsed on the cool, clean, sun-dried porch in front of the kitchen door. A day and night had passed since I had decided to go out and explore the world. The needle stopped quivering. I closed my eyes and wept.

The kitchen door flung open.

Summer's End

JULES had arrived on the Friday twilight boat, and I proudly announced: "Willow is behaving like a normal cat, finally; she took off around noon for a walk. . . . But I'm getting a little nervous, she hasn't shown up yet, and you know how she likes her dinner on time. What do you think? Should we go out looking for her?

"She'll be back. She's a cat whether you or she thinks so or not, and a cat usually finds its way home."

"Usually? It's a new home, and she's so nervous and delicate."

By nine o'clock we were out looking, calling, with the help of a feeble old flashlight. Does anyone ever have a bushy-tailed flashlight around when they need it? We were out for hours, whistling and calling. She had disappeared.

"She's met someone," Jules said. "This is fruitless. Let's go home."

Walking back to the cottage—it must have been midnight—I stopped dead in my tracks. "How irresponsible of us! We should have had her fixed before we came here. How could we have not thought about that?"

"Was she in heat this week?" His tone was critical, edgy, and he was very tired from a hot week in the city. It was all my fault not to have noticed.

"I don't know, she wasn't dripping, as far as I know. . . . Come to think of it, she did let out some whines in the past few days, but I thought it was because she was angry with me and the piano. She hates the sound of the electric piano; it hurts her ears."

"Too late to worry about it now. Anyway, if she's not ready and willing, it won't happen. Fire Island cats aren't dead-end kids," he joked, most inappropriately, I thought.

"She's lost. I know it, she's terrified and lost, gone. . . . We'll never see her again, she'll just curl up and die in the grass somewhere, or . . ." I could see her tiny gray body walking aimlessly on the midnight, deserted beach, walking, walking east to the end of the island, where Europe began. Unless! huge Dobermans, let out to pee, saw her first! I was inconsolable.

That night I dreamed I had misplaced a child, I couldn't find it, didn't know what nursery, what room I had left it in. I woke in panic, fell off to sleep again, and continued the nightmare: A living room as large as a ballroom was filled with people coming and going. In the middle of it sat a green-skinned torso, a sculpture of a child. Someone had brought it and placed it in the center of the room, and it sat, eyes lowered, in its own absolute quiet—an astonishingly beautiful piece of encrusted antiquity. The fragile yet strong presence of the sculpture of a child evoked like music: Something had been made, something had been lost, buried, something had been exhumed only to sit accusingly in the middle of the vast room.

As I slept, the vast subliminal sound of the

ocean must have been an accompaniment to my dream, an intoning basso profundo of a hundred rabbis swaying back and forth about the inevitability, the power of Jehovah that must be borne, even if He chose that a love be lost as a test of one's endurance.

I woke the next morning, in pieces. I didn't take kindly to losing things I loved, a hundred rabbis or an equal number of popes notwithstanding. None of them had the guts to rise up in anger against the random, the illogical, cruel reality of Him.

The morning sun, and no Willow.

She had missed two meals already. Meticulous about her timing, she must be dead.

We went out looking again, knocking on doors now. It was daytime and perfectly normal to knock on doors. There were no cats in the immediate vicinity of the cottage that we had remembered seeing, so she must have gone far afield.

Except . . . knock, knock . . . a ray of light: People we knew slightly, many walks to the east of us. They had a black-and-white male cat, they told us. "Not to worry, he's been neutered."

"Come to think of it, they said, "he hasn't

been around for a day, but he's a gentle, sweet cat; maybe he's showing yours the island. He's been coming here with us for years, he knows every inch of it. You know cats. . . ." They laughed at our distress.

"The only problem is," I said, "Willow isn't a cat."

They looked at me strangely but invited us in for coffee.

In late afternoon, between chords on the electric piano, I heard muffled weeping. I flung open the kitchen door.

"Willow! You found your way back!" A wretched, muddy bit of gray fluff looked up at me, put her head on my shoe, gave a shudder that rippled through her body like a sudden tumbler, and went limp. Lying at my feet was a tiny catastrophe . . . at the moment more devastating than if the African-Arabian landmasses had finally plowed into Europe. "What on earth has happened to your tail!?"

We rushed her off the island to a vet on the mainland. He sewed her tail back together, shot her full of antibiotics, and warned us to keep her quiet and clean or there might have to be an amputation if the stitches didn't work.

Willow was traumatized. Lost, found, over the water, surgery, back over the water in a boat with its terrifying engine throbbing. She spent the rest of the summer indoors and mostly in the closet. Fortunately her tail healed, but forever after had a crook at the end of it, a flagging little crook; but better a crook than half a tail. When she did come out of the closet, she spent hours on the screened-in porch, looking out always with a great, silent tension, her body in an immobile state of quiver, with just the slightest stir in her eyes, looking, looking, like a deer in the shadows of November, its totality programmed to expect danger, the smell of a hunter and his gun. It took us half the summer to figure out what Willow in the closet was all about. She would disappear into it, rummage and go quiet, and sleep for hours if the electric piano was twanging. When I finally parted the clothes to see where she was one day, I discovered she had found an empty shoe box, removed the cover, pulled one of Jules's shirts from its hanger, and lined the box with it. A flash of a thought occurred to me: It was Jules's odor she wanted commingled with her own, not mine, for the future events that were going to happen to her. The secret was out. She looked up at me from the dark, her opal eyes blazing: Yes, births again! And she had chosen the place—the back of this ridiculous little closet with its curtain for a door, smelling of sea-damped wood, and it was all our fault for bringing her here in the first place.

I was filled with dismay, for she could have no idea that we weren't going to be in the cottage for her delivery. She was so brilliant, but not about ordinary physical Time. We would be back in the city . . . and knowing her obsessive, ritualistic ways, she would be completely disoriented.

Willow's silent accusations—her pregnancy was our fault—filled the cottage with gloom, but my composing with words and notes went on, and I think I envied her. Her fate was to languish in the closet this particular summer. Mine was to live with a familiar devil at my elbow, the devil who comes when you "create." I don't remember the time he first materialized in my life, but I do remember feeling almost relieved. I bowed to inevitability, for I had heard: When you imagine yourself Ruler of the Word, however small your kingdom, he's an enemy to expect. But I hardly dreamed he'd come and never go away. When I work, he's everywhere! In my bed, under me, on top of me. . . . The grand gourmand of foreplay, unshaven, crumpled, he doesn't even brush his teeth! Every moment of my fantasies, he's there, laughing in the silence, shouting for his dinner! He tells me I'm ungrateful, that it's not with everyone he burrows in for good.

"For good?" I scream. (He taught me how to scream.)

He finally admits to why he stays. "To bring you to your knees, and my ransom is The Truth." (He's big with capital T's.) "I want The Truth from you," he threatens.

"That's impossible, I don't have *The* Truth, I only have my own!"

And so he stays, watching me crawl through muck like a starving primordial with tail, thrashing about to find the phrase *delizioso,* as smooth and light as double virgin olive oil; the shock of recognition; the grand design; words so True, so Right, so

Virile that they bleed when pricked! (Emerson said that of Montaigne.)

Would that I could exorcise him back to hell, but I never owned a cross, or cracked one page of the Cabala. And so he stays, wherever I happen to be (and working)—because the ransom is too high. The cottage was no exception, small as it was, with the electric piano on the porch, its couches filled with notebooks and papers, Willow in her sullen retreat in the closet, that devil at my elbow. . . . In spite of it all, I did some good work that summer, if not the whole Truth, at least a few good songs for a musical that was never to be; but I didn't know that then.

As in all past summers, the leave-taking day meant a walk to the ocean to say a final good-bye to the vast horizon, a last gaze at the waves, a last deep breath. Willow, not having been outside since her catastrophic foray, suddenly found herself being scooped up in my arms, to accompany us. She shivered and fought, her claws digging into my arms for dear life, all the way to the landing on the dunes. But then she looked out and I knew she was looking with us, maybe even enjoying the wind on her face. Her body relaxed; she recognized that we were partaking in some sort of serious observance, voices speaking back and forth to one another, the ocean and beach to us; we, to them: Go home from the littered shore, we are summer's end, thrown up, dead, crashed against a sandbar, winter-colored, arrow to the snow, tail to the sun-fat summer. Leave us to the caw-caw calling on the frosty water when you are gone. . . .

With an intrigued Willow, we ventured onto the beach and walked to the water's edge. Her back arched as a wave came in; it eased as the wave left, but safe in my arms, she channeled no fear, even when I bent down to pick up a shell: Yes, bend down once more, to out Hiroshiga-blue-tipped shells, feel our black, perfect fans. Turn our rough, broken, mother-of-pearl wings to the other side of perfection, to our dark, shell-wing cry. Here we are, crashed by the storm last night, by a full-moon tide—our pride lies deep in the sea now. So do not supervise the burial. Go home, you scavengers of corpses. Let us rest in the gentle wind.

We turned our backs and left, with not a peep out of Miss Willow, who was busy sniffing the shells in my hand. She knew a ceremony when she saw one.

BACK HOME

A Tidal Wave of Events

BACK in the apartment in September, the first thing we did after unpacking was to find a box, line it with one of Jules's shirts, place it in the large, walk-in closet in our bedroom, and show it to Willow. Not even a brrrp of acknowledgment. She ignored the closet like a plague. I feared she would. She had chosen the Fire Island cottage closet for her delivery and would have none of this dislocation; she'd show us.

It was a comforting return to her favorite haunts again—the window seats overlooking the park, the lady's chair—as if we had never left, as if nothing were imminent, except for her eating enough to feed an army in her belly, which got bigger by the week, much bigger than in her first pregnancy.

A day came when Willow was not to be found. We looked everywhere, even on the tops of cabinets. We knew she couldn't jump, what with her heaviness, but we searched up high anyway, stupidly frantic.

"This is ridiculous," Jules said. "How can you lose a pregnant cat who refuses to have anything to do with going out?"

We looked in drawers, closets, behind the stove. We opened the door and walked up and down the three floors of the brownstone.

No Willow.

She had programmed not only herself but us, so successfully, about her aversion to the closet in our bedroom that it had never entered our minds to look for her there! But there she was, in the box . . . and her delivery had begun. One tiny bit of kitten life lay squirming on Jules's shirt, and she was trying to push out another. Should we watch or leave? We decided to give her privacy.

About fifteen minutes later she was at the bedroom door and let out a yowl.

"What is it, Willow?"

She walked back into the closet, and we followed. There was a second kitten, noticeably smaller than the first, but squirming. She got back into the box and we left again. A moment later, there she was at the door, looking up at Jules and yowling louder. He walked her back to the closet, she got into her box, but when he tried to leave, she cried out.

"She wants me to stay with her, that's what's going on," Jules called out to me. "Bring me a stool or something." In the next half hour it became very clear that she was not having an easy birth. I sat on our bed as Jules reported to me from inside the closet. She was letting him feel her stomach, touch her, and stroke her; she wasn't washing off the first two kittens very well, because she seemed in great discomfort, he reported.

"I'm moving them close to her mouth, but she doesn't seem to want to clean them or isn't able, I don't know which. There are more in her, that's for sure; I can feel them."

"More? How many more? In that little body? What should we do, call the vet?"

"Here comes another one!" Jules cried out, and then, in almost a whisper to himself, "She's definitely in trouble, poor thing. But she's beginning to wash them."

"Don't touch the little ones," I warned. "Your smell will confuse them. I'm coming in, too; I don't care if she wants me in the closet or not! I have to see what's going on."

The birthing-closet had an ashen feel. Willow looked spent. Jules and I looked at each other. How could we bring her and them to the vet's in the middle of all of this? There was nothing we could do but watch and try to help.

Jules kept stroking her forehead, and she seemed to want the connection. Suddenly she became convulsed with pain and pushed out the next one, barely a full term kitten at all. With what seemed like her last bit of strength, Willow sniffed at it, licked it, and collapsed. Four! "Let's leave her alone now," Jules said. "She'll come to and do what she's supposed to. . . ."

As far as I was concerned, the closet was not only ashen, it was an unsanitary, ill-lit obstetrics ward, puerperal fever was raging; Semmelweis was hard at work in his laboratory, but he hadn't discovered antisepsis as a concept yet. I voiced my hysteria: Willow would die in childbirth!

"Don't be an ass," Jules said. That meant he was as apprehensive as I was.

We left the closet, went into the living room, and waited, trusting that nature, in Willow's complex structure as a cat, would prevail. All would be well. Happy ending. And we'd be faced with, how many? four, five cats? They would all survive and we'd be faced *again* with the task of finding Freudian-oriented adoptive parents. An hour went by. I made coffee, Jules read, we peeked at Willow washing her kittens, we left, we waited. She came into the kitchen, looked up at the stove, and demanded warm milk for herself; then she returned to the box.

Suddenly, a shocking scream of pain. We both went running. Willow had ejected another kitten and it was quite dead, an actual embryo. Now she left the box and refused to return, no matter how we coaxed and placed her into it, time after time. Jules had removed the dead one, small as a sparrow, and taken it to the cellar garbage can. By the end of the day we had to admit that something strange and terrible had happened to her; she was rejecting her litter and we were left with four tiny, wet infants mewling for milk.

Willow retired to the linen drawer in mortification and wouldn't come out, not even for food.

From then on, nothing mattered except trying to feed the kittens with eyedroppers, without success. Their tiny squeaks of hunger became so intolerable that we placed them on a pillow, stuffed them into a pillowcase, and hoping to prevent a surge of deaths, we ran to the nearest vet we could find, who agreed to try to feed them for a few days. But the following day we received a call telling us that the vet (A for effort) had thrown up his hands; there were too many cats in the world anyway, enough was enough, his staff was too busy. What was absolutely indicated now (which we should have thought about after her first pregnancy), the vet suggested: "Your cat should have a hysterectomy, but let her rest up first."

When we had come back home after delivering her litter to the vet, Willow was waiting for us at the door, something she never did—it was too servile. But that day she was there, to read our faces. After the vet's call the next day, there was no doubt that she perceived the fate of her litter.

"Well, that's that, try to close the door on that one," she said, and walked back to the privacy of the linen drawer—her lavender-smelling, Wamsutta-flowered hermitage—for full retreat, meditation, and penitent review as well as postpartum depression. There was no question she was depressed: Her fur hung, her eyes drooped, hormones of worthlessness seemed to have robbed her of all wish to continue unless she could rationalize her way out of what had happened. If she couldn't forgive herself and forget, her mind would snap completely from the tests meted out by the Absolute. It had had no right to force her, and force it was, into the suckling, selfless love-giving role again. She was not meant for such use or test; she knew she was meant to be a virgin queen, a ruler, a thinker, philosopher, maybe even a writer. Motherhood once was enough, and she had done it magnificently, hadn't she, the first time?

Little did we know that the tidal wave of events beginning with her disappearance for a day on the island, her pregnancy-debacle that followed, her slow recovery . . . had not ended. It would swell to even greater proportion before it broke, subsided, and ended its rampage.

Call the best cat doctor in town. Get his fee for a hysterectomy. It was astronomical. Should we use the large animal hospital that had been highly recommended by all sorts of feline-lovers? "No question about it," we had been assured, it had "the newest technological gadgets, even an intensive-care unit for cardiac patients."

No problem, we imagined. First, we'd whisper in Willow's ear what was going to happen. Then we'd take her, cuddle her, love her, say good-bye to her, leave her, and voilà! retrieve her after it was all over. There was no reason for anxiety, we told ourselves; stop anthropomorphizing, it's an animal, not a human, after all . . .

But this was Willow! Had we ever taken

George Sand, Eleanor of Aquitaine, Catherine de Medici, Elizabeth I for a hysterectomy?

First of all, we never counted on Willow not being able to tolerate a hospital ward, medicine for the commonality, a zoo for the sick. She went into shock.

There once was a beautiful human duchess (her country of origin escapes me) who found herself in the middle of the Spanish Civil War in the late 1930s—the harbinger of World War II—with Hitler and Mussolini testing their new weapons and tactics against the Spanish republic, in support of General Franco and his fascist legions. The duchess was being evacuated from a battle zone, in an overcrowded train filled with peasants and revolutionary soldiers. The journey took days. She refused to avail herself of the facility used by the commonality. She would not, she would not! use the train's toilet and pee where the peasants peed! So she held it in, poor lady, held it in for her class, her code, her generations of aristocracy; and she became paler and paler, until she was so violently ill, she had to be carried off the train on a stretcher, her body filled with poisons, her bladder about to burst, and her kidney functions destroyed. She was placed on the embankment, where she died, just another body to join all the other bodies left to rot in the sun during that dreadful war. But die for a cause she did, and the peasants and soldiers on the train shook their heads in wonderment.

Willow also had made a decision to die because of the surroundings she found herself in. The day we went to take her home after her operation, we were confronted by a Willow with a festering, incompetently treated incision, and she was suffering from severe infection and dehydration. Jules turned into a raging bull, and I felt like fainting. She lay in the back of a cage, soaked and consumed with fever. When she saw us, weak as she was, she snarled. Was this the result of an ordinary, everyday hysterectomy? we demanded to know.

"That's not our cat! That's not the cat we brought here!" I cried. "What have you people done to her?"

"She won't drink anything. She refuses water," they said.

"What about her wound? Why is it infected? Who's responsible?" Jules demanded to know. He was answered with a shrug.

"We could put her on an IV," they said, "but we figured you wouldn't want all that fuss and expense. She's not a pedigreed one, after all. . . ."

We looked at them with amazement, and I could feel Jules becoming litigious, and more so by the second. If he didn't run to the phone and hire a lawyer, I thought he would at the least punch someone. I grabbed him by the arm. "Of course the little bitch won't drink anything," I exploded. "She doesn't drink water! She only drinks milk if she sees it being warmed up in her little yellow pot! Go home and get the pot, and I'm staying right here until you get back!"

The hospital staff thought us quite mad, but Jules *did* go, and did come back with the little yellow pot. We made them fill it with warm milk. I placed it beside her in the cage, and she drank, by God . . . she drank like a sand-whipped desert wanderer stumbling on a Grade B movie oasis. She had gotten herself down to a few ounces of fluff and bone, but even with death so near, it had been necessary for her to act out: This is who

I am, and I will die for it, the justice of myself as I see it. You should never have
brought me here to suffer these indignities!
her eyes said after she had done with the
drinking. She snarled at us again.

The attendants said she was a nasty, unmanageable animal; she had even scratched
a nurse. *Willow,* snarling and unmanageable?
We decided not to leave her in that cage for
another second. We grabbed her and said we
were taking her home to die. But that isn't
what we did at all. We flew crosstown in a
cab to that best cat doctor in town, the ex-
pensive one, where we should have taken her
in the first place, our impossible duchess.

Without warning or appointment, we
stormed into the doctor's office with an animal *in extremis.* The nurse saw our need immediately and without a word brought us to
the famous one. We were wanting to explain
what had happened to her, but he waved our
words away and began to examine, palpate,
undo the filthy, pus-stained bandage, spray
the incision with antibiotics, inject more antibiotics. He gently but tightly wound a gir-
dle-bandage around her belly, told us to
pray, and then said, "Who's responsible for

this butchering, lousy medicine? Don't tell me; I don't want to know."

We told him anyway. "A sweet little animal," he said. "It'll be touch and go for a few days, so try to keep her quiet, off the floor. Watch her like a hawk." He popped a pill down her throat, and Willow made not one sign of protest. She had been nothing if not cooperative. When it was all over, she gave him her number-one full gaze, causing the doctor to say, "Amazing eyes you have, little one. Chin up. I hope you make it." And he gave her head a loving stroke. We told him about her having scratched a nurse at the hospital and that they said she was nasty and unmanageable.

"Of course! And wouldn't we be, under the same circumstances? There must have been another ingredient, though, to make her so mad. Some animals, just like people, are more sensitive than others, more definite in their spirits, even call it a higher IQ." He smiled. "This young lady is a special something, and she knows it, you can tell by the gaze. She has a big dose of Burmese in her genes; long, dainty body; tiny paws; firm chin; head not so long as the Siamese; long, thin tale ending in a point. . . . What happened with the tail?" We told him and he laughed. "A slight kink is permissible."

The man was a lover, no question about it; a lover and a humanist. Standing over Willow was an oldish, wispy, but sinewy man, with learning, listening, thinking lines all over his face. He had been gently touching the parts of Willow's body that showed Burmese with such admiration and affection that I knew there was a healing process going on at that very moment. Heal wound, heal pride, heal spirit, kazamm! We were in the presence of a gifted one. What is there about a true virtuoso that changes the air, fills it with immediacy, an impetuous embrace, a budding process, a lack of cringe, an absence of the petty? Prideful honoring of discipline and experience hard-gained—all of it was in the examining room, swirling around the seasoned practitioner of hope.

What is there about even a cranky, irascible genius of a human; manipulating, selfish Picasso; a mad Dali; an imperious, impatient Martha Graham; a private, humble Einstein; a skittish, highly neurotic Horowitz? *They transform the air.* Henry Adams once wrote about meeting the poet Swinburne at a social gathering in London. He didn't know who Swinburne was, whether poet or banker, but the bearing, the talk of the man (they were both young then) permeated the room with an individual, idiosyncratic brilliance that Adams was never to erase from his mind. On another level, to be sure, but with the same brilliance, the doctor who had urged Willow to heal had had the same air around him.

She would have died, otherwise. And she knew it. Her body was filled with appreciation and thanks. But Willow being Willow, she was also swearing inside: "Idiots, you! This is where I should have been brought in the first place. Penny-wise and pound-foolish!" As for the Absolute Peaceful Hand, it was nothing but vengeance—a lesson well taught, she had decided. Vengeance must be met with vengeance, and vengeance meant she must live. The doctor lifted her off the examining table, and as he handed her to us, she looked at him and gave him one of her special, trilling brrps. Her elegant self had been restored.

After several days of enforced rest, she minced about the house like a vindicated ruler after a failed palace coup, bearing her tight girdle of a bandage and the difficulty in walking as ribbons of honor, and slowly forgiving us for our sin of penny-wise and pound-foolish.

I was filled with a fury that wouldn't go away. I had heard the doctors and nurses say I wasn't pedigreed, so what was all the fuss about, whether I drank or didn't drink liquids? They never looked at the incision or changed the bandage, so I showed them in the only way I could—I scratched and snarled—that they were guilty of not caring.

I heard them plan my death by injection, and how they would let Her and Him know by telephone that somehow I wasn't able to recover.

I saw how they treated the purebreeds as against the so-called mongrels. Alley cat, indeed! That's what they called me. I knew now, in sudden maturity, what the psychosis of poverty was all about, the apathy that kills, which I would not have if I had not had the experience firsthand—

a hospital ward in all its horror. I was just a name and number on a cage.

And I learned another very important thing: He and She had cried for me, done everything to save me. They had brought me to that doctor with the old eyes, whose hands felt like the touch of the Absolute itself. And I learned, like a miracle, that I was not reentered into this world to learn how to be a victim. I had to learn about the power of love and what happens when love is absent. I became a political animal for the rest of my life.

By the end of 1962, Willow had become a different *person,* I swear; as if she had turned into an inveterate letter-to-the-editor writer, a world worrier, a radical in a gray mink coat. She truly developed a love for Bach, Mozart, Chopin; and it was as if she had discovered the essays of Montaigne, Schopenhauer, Bacon, and had become a serious student of Hegel and Marx. If she had begun to compare the various translations of Aeschylus's *Oresteia,* I would have thrown up my hands.

It was a very different Willow. There were

times when she sat, not like a cat; lay, not like a cat; and the times were more human than cat. She moved from room to room, on the ready for people, ideas, words, music, so tuned in to our rhythms, it was eerie. She made herself alert to everything that mattered in the household, with her ears cocked, her opal eyes focusing not on movement, as a cat, but on a moment defined by communication through word.

It was also becoming clear (in retrospect) why she had sat on print, why certain books were never opened to the page you left them.

And who knew why she had to sit next to the typewriter hour after hour! As long as you could take it, so could she—interfering with your hands when she felt that something needed reconsideration, a rewrite. Who knew that she was learning and stealing like mad? One day I almost felt like stuffing her in my tote bag, to accompany me to the Museum of Modern Art, so she could see for herself Picasso's *Guernica*—the twentieth century's genius scream against war, betrayal, the absence of love.

* * *

The year 1963 was a year fraught with distress, not only for Willow; the country she lived in had as good as declared a second Civil War. The civil rights movement, like a sleepy volcano, blew off its cone, and the hot lava was beginning to flow down, leaving no southern city or town unscathed, no northern community without guilt.

Willow discovered television. It started with *The Mickey Mouse Club* and later *Sesame Street,* to which she became addicted for the rest of her life, the way many highly intelligent people sneak-watch *Dallas,* and if they miss one episode, they've *got* to call some other intelligent person, and the secret is out. In the 1960s she became addicted to news-watching, her tail switching violently, her mouth open as police dogs broke up riots, their barks as frightening as if they were in her quiet bedroom. She sat stock still with us, her back rippling with attention, watching white-hooded Klansmen streak across the screen, rednecks on horseback, bodies being dragged along the street, billy clubs swinging because black children wanted to go to school, or their parents and grandparents wanted to vote. And sometimes the screen would become fogged with tear gas, at which point she had had enough and stormed out of the room. We could hear her rattling about in the kitchen, banging her food plate against her milk saucer to remind us that it was time to eat and remember the good things. But there were black mothers for whom it must have been more difficult to remember the good things. Black mothers whose little girls were killed by a bomb blast in a Birmingham church. They sat keening at their kitchen tables:

Cool my little one for me, God. While she waits, rest her head on the hip of heaven. She'll be safe there, where everyone can see her. Tell her, I don't know how our hands broke apart. Ask her, was dying scary without Mama? Tell her, I'm walkin' fast to meet her. But while she waits, you're gonna rest her head on the hip of heaven, O Lord, where everyone can see her, or I ain't gonna pray no more!

And other unusual events began to image themselves in the air of the 1960s. The young began to grow their hair long, bedeck themselves with flowers, writhe and groan in love clasps and rock beats in the soft, cloudy, sweet smell of pot—rebellion against the madness.

Watching Willow strut away from the doings of humans, to escape into the silence of cat, how often through the years had I wished enviously for the magic of such a switch off.

The next summer, it was Fire Island again, and the little white cottage. Willow took it bravely; she simply never went out. ("I don't in the city, I won't here! I'm a house cat—end of discussion.") We didn't suggest or coax. She had reached the height of her beauty that would remain unchanged, little could we imagine, for almost twenty-one years—sleek gray, glistening whiskers, incredible white lashes, and her eyes were unreal jewels. She did sit for hours at the kitchen's screened door, however, and one day, in the late afternoon, she emitted an ear-splitting scream that repeated itself to such amazing decibels, it could have been the scream of a lioness. I thought she had gone quite mad. On the other side of the screen door stood a grinning black-and-white cat. She swore obscenities, shook with fury. "Get him! Jail him! Don't psychoanalyze him, kill him!"

Her monumental rage made it evident to me, beyond a shadow of a doubt, that here was "the perpetrator," the biter of tails, the father of her misbegotten litter. Was *he* the black-and-white cat our neighbors had said they'd neutered? Should I tell them it didn't work? Or would I be guilty of a false accusation? Would they take Willow's word for it? I did! They'd think me completely pixilated. Forget it, I said to myself.

The poor animal slunk away in unperceiving dumbness, with a backward look that said: "Well, if that's the way you want it . . . I only came by to say hello."

It took her hours to recover from the spirit fall, the yowl of all cats having exploded inside her. She retired to the closet with the curtain for a door, and I'm sure, ruminated at great length about her gentleman caller, a reminder of what she really was—a cat.

FILLING
AND FALLING

Spiritual Love/ Theater

BACKWARD looks are unsettling; they can't help but evaluate and judge, often severely. But unlike old pages of writing found again, maybe even worthy of editing, years cannot be edited, except by one's ability to lie or deny. They can never be altered, only questioned: What was learned? What madness made me? What an amazing turn of events! Who *was* the I who took that road?

Each of the seven years following our last summer on Fire Island was a time of change. The one unchanging element was the presence of Miss Willow. She was the constant, the utterly dependable, with her beauty asleep on top of the piano, or her irresistible curves settled into the lady's chair, or in the crook of my arm at night.

The house, the marriage, the child, work —all could change at a moment's notice. Except Willow—her demands for proper meal-time, the little yellow pot filled with milk warming on the stove, her insistence on a daily immaculate pan (it had to be flushed after each use, and if we were not there to do so, she simply withheld her kidney and bowel functions until our return). And if it seemed a bit eccentric for Jules or me to look at our watches in the middle of a business meeting out in the world, and think, I have to get home, Willow's probably holding it in —*that* was the reality of the constant. You couldn't be casual with Willow; you couldn't say, Oh, she's a cat, she can wait, cats don't have the same sense of time. Not Willow, an executive who ran a tight ship, and if we behaved ourselves, we could count on a job with all the side benefits, for life. It was also like having a forever child, a Peter Pan, the spirit that never grows up. (Though that wasn't quite true in her case—only her little body never seemed to change.)

Not so with our son, Chucky, who became Chuck, no longer little boy, but boy. His growth was as astonishing as watching the metamorphosis of seed to flower to fruit, through stop-motion photography. It seemed like only one microsecond before that he had sat playing on the beach, with his little brown back innocently facing the waves, piling the sand into tumbling spires. Crabs were kings and clams were vassals; sea glass, beach plums, polished stones he commanded with an "I want thee!" His childhood minutes hung by their toes, so cocky, so sure of themselves. (How expansive and indulgent time is, with bright new pendulums, shining, free of history, sins and sums.)

And suddenly he's playing an oboe and owns a dirty, trusty baseball glove. And suddenly Willow isn't dashing away from his unpredictable little feet but is curling herself up on his lap, and he's learning the sensuous feel of stroking, petting, loving the vulnerable. Boys who own baseball gloves and wear smelly sneakers don't kiss easily, even parents whose knees they used to hug and noses they kissed with abandon. But Chuck could kiss Willow, even on her soft little belly; it always took her aback but she allowed it, dissolving into a giggling duchess. She *played* with Chuck and never did with us. I think she taught herself how to do a somersault just to make him laugh. Only a fabulist could explain how she knew the gymnastics of somersaulting. She had never seen one done until she did it—put her head between her legs, rolled herself under and over, perfect as a wheel, and stood up with a flushed ta-da! At first she performed them for Chuck alone and we didn't believe his account of them. Then she began to do them for us when she felt impish, and even for our guests, if she liked them and the atmosphere in the living room. She would make her entrance—like Fred Astaire walking down a street and suddenly breaking into a dance routine—execute two somersaults and walk off to astonished applause. It was a peculiar tic of happiness and very vaudeville.

The duchess had a sly sense of humor. She did her somersaults well into her old age, throwing us into fits of laughter, as if a venerated character actress at a party given in her honor suddenly takes it into her head to astonish the stuffy and mime slipping on a banana peel.

About those seven years of change Willow definitely had something to say in that "I write in the air" style of hers, ineffable yet pointed, that lethal combination of arrogance mixed with the wisdom of the silent ones:

Those years got to the heart of her—what She could do, couldn't do; what She did and shouldn't have, not to mention what the Absolute Peaceful Hand had in store for her. Cancer of the mind, then body, both of which she recovered from, thank the A.P.H.

In truth, my beloved She had me worried to death for a while. I amaze myself. I have never used or thought the word *beloved* before. I would never want her to know, not until after I die. Maybe she won't even know it then, if she can't decipher my writing.

What the Absolute gives always leaves humans unnerved and stunned, as if what happens to them is the first time it's ever

happened. Their innocence is what makes
me so curious about humans. Sometimes
they remind me of balloons, the way they
blow themselves up in expectation, float off
in rapture, lose their air, shrink, wrinkle,
collapse, blow themselves up again, and
start over, filled with that innocence again.
And fear. Not about dying but about
everything. The flimsy sickness I call it.
Dying should be the only fear, not
knowing where you are going again. So
what if it's not a "far, far better rest that I
go to, than I have ever known"? I had to
laugh when I heard her read that to the
boy one day. The hero of the book made
them cry with relief, the way he was so
sure he was going to a better place after he
was guillotined. Maybe the perfect rest is
being a *salamander!* That's why I laughed.
You just have to leave it to the Absolute.
You just have to Be. Everything else knows
that, except humans. Granted, maybe being
human means you're the only animal that
can fill itself, fall itself . . . but why are
they always so funny, so surprised about
the brain and soul given to their species?
You'd think they would have gotten used

to it after so many thousands of years of filling and falling?

No.

In those years Willow referred to, with my "filling and falling," *Mrs. Godolfin Says "No"* was put aside because I was chosen to write the score for a play by Eugene O'Neill that needed forty minutes of music: *Marco Millions.* It was to be one of the plays presented in the first year of Lincoln Center's dream—to become *the* American repertory theater—as well as plays by Arthur Miller and S. N. Behrman. I was in a state of complete euphoria and fear for the six months of composing, rehearsing, working with actors who weren't trained in *speak-sing,* that lift into fantasy and heightened feeling when words are imbedded in music for the effect of *total* theater—play, emotion, dance, poetry. But we tried—the actors; the director, José Quintero; the orchestra; and myself—and we revived an atypical O'Neill play that was almost a musical, that hadn't been produced since 1928. And I learned in one big gasp about *professional,* top-of-the-class theater, about sweating palms, talents, jealousies, deadlines, dress rehearsals when everything fell apart, temper tantrums, white-knuckled previews, actors in trouble, actors soaring on beautiful moments, the rapt silence of audiences meaning things were *working;* the restlessness and coughing that meant boredom; then the emotional vacuum of opening night, the empty stomach and pounding head, the naked embarrassment of "What have we done!?" The unparalleled excitement of a curtain rising. What a way to learn theater, to be thrown, not into a potbellied stove, but into the furnace of a steel mill! Get tempered or die.

I knew I had done well. I had written an unusual score. O'Neill's political fantasy play was about Marco Polo, the ugly Westerner who invaded ancient China and saw none of its beauty and wisdom, only the material things he could bring back to Italy, like spaghetti, silkworms, and firecrackers. I wrote modern music to be played on ancient instruments. Lush, strange-sounding, interpretive music, always with the modern, satiric voice of the playwright leading me. What an honor to sit with the ghost of O'Neill in a work session, hearing the tone of his voice in objection, praise, suggestions, and there were many. He was a most kind collaborator, not cranky or impatient or ego-driven except for the work to be realized the way he had envisioned it, and maybe even delighted with a fullness he could never have imagined, the way his director, Quintero, had brought the play to a new life. Minor but fascinating O'Neill, the critics called it? According to Quintero, there could never be such a thing as minor when it came to O'Neill, and I agreed.

Filling and falling. I fell in love with José Quintero. While watched by Jules, under-standing but jealous; by Chuck, respectful of his celebratedness, as if Mom had a new baseball hero; by Nick Tsacrios, José's be-mused companion; and by Willow, who al-ways chose to be present in the living room when José visited, lest she miss a new epi-sode of my transformation. She always knew when talk was important—she listened and hummed like mad to herself, like the indul-gent wife of the village rabbi who was hardly wiser than she, but her lot, alas, was to re-main respectfully silent.

I adored Quintero's dark, elegiacal "genius"; his dark-stranger Panamanian handsomeness; his raspy, smoke-laden Spanish accent; his long-lashed eyes black as a Mexican well into which a sacrificial virgin would willingly throw herself. Oh, Emily Brontë, creator of dark men, José's birdlike diminutive Castilian mother created one as well, yet Señora Quintero was never awed by what she had made—a glowing talent of theater. If he didn't cook pork chops to her liking, she would pound her little fists on his elbow.

The outward appearance of the "dark stranger" aside, it was his symbiotic connection with the equally stormy, dark New England soul of O'Neill that I loved. José's genius was in capturing the ineffable and wrapping those who worked with him in his own cloak, to unmask the uncoverable, the truth of passion. He was not afraid to bait the bull, to challenge himself and it into a state of outrageous courage. Or he had another way: How to make naked that moment of emotion that protects itself like a wary child? Coax it out into the open with whispers, love, and trust, for those moments make actors like deer standing at the edge of a forest, wondering if it's safe to walk out into the open meadow, he would say.

I fell in love with this virtuoso of theater magic. And I think, he with me, though not with my fantasies. But love flowed back and forth, so necessary when people are working together to make the elusive real. Every theater project is as nuttily redolent with emotion, romance of every stripe and possibility, as a cruise ship sailing in a full-moon week. Because the act of collaboration means the act of loving if it is to mean anything. "Darling! Darling!" Wherefore comes that cry if not from theater people clinging to each other, vulnerable as nudists or a clutch of shipwrecked sailors in a lifeboat? Not to forget that so much loving can suddenly flip to the other side of the coin—anger, jealousy, and murder. Then "Darling!" becomes so versatile everyone knows it means "Kill!"

It was a new kind of love for me—one with fences—mutual admiration and no touching. I was married and a mother. José was a homosexual.

Lest I sink into a spell (of loving José), morals and sexual persuasion stood over me like towering golem dressed in nuns' garb.

So dream like one who longs to touch the
moon, I bade myself. Lo and behold! The
moon *was* touched—just a few years later—
by men in space suits! Proving that *real*
moons can be touched. But the satellite of
the heart, in certain cases, can never be.

I had steered myself into a dangerous
promontory, imagining the safety of shore-
lines that weren't there. There was something so reminiscent in my pain. What was
it? Ah, yes, the prickly-pear years of adolescence. Wounded by them again, after all the
in-between time of maturity. What fun. To
adore again. How idiotic. How gaily irresponsible to eat the mushroom and fall, fall,
filling myself as I fell.

José taught me to like myself a little more,
to dare to think: Hey, you're good when the
wind blows right sometimes. I fell in love
with his soul for that. He treated me as if I
were a Henry James heroine, someone to be
both cosseted *and* tested, encouraged, someone whose inner strengths could be formida-
ble, as fragile and quaking as the outer shell
appeared. I had, hadn't I, my advanced degree in Quaking? He made me laugh that I
was friable, easily crumbled like the crust of

good bread (not crumbled like a human in distress); and the outer signs promised a succulent bite into a good roll. He taught me to trust my instincts. For that I will love him forever. To this day, sometimes when I work, wondering about the process of making it *sound,* wondering if the mumblings in my head could have any worth for someone else's, his eyes are in the room, signaling, "Go on!"

Punishing Love/
Repairing Love

PAPA died, my first love.

The rest would have happened anyway—
not in the same toppling way, but some re-
definition of marriage would have arched its
head in warning, like a threatened snake before it bites.

Papa—my original love. I thought I handled his death as well as any ever-to-be-un-
resolved longing to be loved, the loss of the
original imprint. I had freed myself of so
much of the childhood memory that had
haunted me—the ghost with the infrequent
smile, its pat on my head as passionate as
copulation (the little girl's wish). *Taboo* is a

brilliant invention to brake reality from careening into incest. Otherwise, Oedipus gropes his way through life, blind; or Phaedre goes stark, raving mad into suicide. Taboo is only a mechanical device that protects the outside walls from crashing in. The glittering-eye unconscious of fathers and daughters, mothers and sons (buried as deep as the center of Earth, for its own protection) has ever perceived with the eyes of young wantons. The unconscious knows nothing of *Beware!* it takes a lifetime to train it to lie down like a good doggie.

And even then . . .

Up come the patterns cut from the original cloth of loving, and you choose withholding, removed people to love. (As I did all through my college years, before my marriage.)

I chose the indifferent to be hopelessly in love with, and rejected those who loved me without reservation, trick, or shadow. Except two. One I lost in the fog of war, and the other I married. My marriage was a successful conspiracy against my unconscious.

Yet, sometimes it's just the reverse. To make life dangerous and out of control, you give yourself to someone who is insatiable for conquest, without his loving.

After many years of being married, that's what happened, and it was not coincidental that it was the year my father died.

Go for the forbidden, the grudging, but with a new ingredient, amorality. The galloping promiscuity of the times helped. The insidious beat of rock helped. Gyrating hips, sexual, and social revolution were taking the oxygen out of the air of the sixties, and the world was running the mile so fast. . . . Could I imagine entering the competition, me, the New England girl, congenital-virginal, Jamesian heroine of Washington Square? Hell, yes . . . I opened my door to a *really dark* and *interested* stranger. All discretion fell away, the ability to smell danger, dig an imposter, a spurious Othello. The black man I allowed to entice me into infidelity wasn't a good man; in his head he wore a belt with notches on it, each notch a white woman he had gotten to bed. Never you mind, my heart said. I pitied him for his anger. I was omnipotent, my love would smooth away the injustice, I would have his child, I was still young enough. . . . My fantasies went logically wild. Had not my mother the Communist, adorer of Paul Robeson, and my father, the socialist doctor who had dedicated his life to the dream of a freed humanity, had they not trained me for this crossover into the oppressed black world, to live it firsthand? To go the whole way, beyond where they had gone? To watch an elegantly suited black man try to hail a cab at midnight and it wouldn't stop, though empty, and to cry for his shame and anger? How would my protected, shallow white mind manage the real battle—of bus seats, restaurants, my child rejected from a white schoolroom, toilets for whites only, not for *my* child? I reeled with the excitement of sharing the injustice, relieving my white guilt. My chance had come, to live in the real world of pain in the mid-to-late-sixties, not in the cloister of the Freudian's.

The early sixties, with their first anguished cries of *Black is beautiful,* this is our fight, we'll go it alone, we don't need you, whitey, to march with us . . . were totally disorienting for whites, who assumed their hands would be grabbed in solidarity. I would never forget a scene from those years in the

living room of a close friend. The talk was
tumbling and good. A well-known black ac-
tor-singer, slowly getting drunk, was holding
forth. I interrupted him in the middle of a
sentence and he spat out in fury: "Go fuck
the moon, white woman! Don't you dare interrupt me! I don't need your fucking mind!"
The room of black and white friends was
stunned into silence. A few years later, my
chance to be close to that world of pain had
come.

Nonsense. *Sharing the injustice* wasn't the
reason. I was raging with a burning fever
from a strain of the Lady Chatterley virus,
when the white cell count plummets and the
immune system lays down its defenses. The
disease is contracted from unconscious longing realized—close contact with male, steel-
mill muscles, a poet in rough trade, the mystery of the unknown, the embrace of a pirate
in the disguise of a gentle man, black *or*
white. I slowly discovered that *my* Othello
not only had a mistress, but at least two
other Desdemonas. He was a disturbed, insatiable and busy man. What a frightening
world out there, with its unleashed uncon-
sciouses bumping against each other like

clouds laden with thunderstorm, lightning flashes hitting everywhere. My house had been hit. It burned down. My house, the house of my father. I had lost my pride.

What world had I left, and was it still there? Chuck was there, Willow was there. Oh, was she there! She wore a permanent look on her face:

I knew what was going on. I saw it with my own eyes. I was shocked. She couldn't hide it from me. Possessed by the devil, is what it was. It made nothing right anymore. No meals on time, people coming and going, voices nasty and funny. She looked the same, but I didn't know her, or want to. So I began to sleep in the boy's room. No more in the crook of her arm. I don't sleep with strangers. I showed her!

Jules was not there, but in my myopic, colossal self-absorption, the thought that he might not be had never occurred to me.

Yet, why should he have been? I was out at night for too many rehearsals; once, away for a whole week. I was abstracted, distant, flushed with secrets and lies. It's amazing how hormones can create instantaneous bloom. Jules saw it all and kept silent, kept the household going. But he was bereft and lonely, and he met someone who saw it on his face, someone he found attractive, someone who said: "Let me make it up to you, whatever it is you've lost, whatever that neurotic, selfish woman, your wife, has done." And soon she was giving him an ultimatum: "You have to make up your mind. You have to leave her if you want a relationship with me."

"I mean, I wanna be around to pick up the pieces/when someone else breaks your heart . . . la, la, la . . . Wanna feel sweet revenge . . ." Jules never sang that song, not even to himself, I think. My best friend wasn't a vengeful or gloating man. He was aghast that our marriage had fallen apart. For a year it had been secrets and lies, making believe the structure, the nest we had built, was intact.

I was so occupied with my own betrayal that I had no idea he was having an affair, until the end of the summer.

Chuck went off to camp. I went to a month-long playwrights' conference at the

Eugene O'Neill Theater Center in Connecticut, and took Willow with me. She and I were going to share a room at an inn. Jules was going to be in Colorado, making a television film. The family dispersed in all directions. My wild fandango was over, but my wounds were still covered with bandages. I had no one to talk with, the kind of talk that heals, that only those who love you no matter what, can share. That was Jules! And there was Willow. She wouldn't talk to me. She was furious, cooped up in one room at the inn, and she didn't like me anymore. I had destroyed stability, the pleasant evenness of hours counted on, I had blown love, the daily grace that keeps a family together, out of the air.

It was 1967. Because of José, I had been part of the O'Neill playwrights' conference since its beginning in 1965, as composer. That first year had been a heady experience, to be part of a dream—an oasis for new American plays to be developed in a benign, caring atmosphere, away from the bitter competition of the marketplace. For writers to live and work on their own pieces with other artists of the theater—directors, stage designers, actors; to see their work realized and be criticized by thoughtful professionals. It was the big, extravagant dream of a theater-lover named George White of Connecticut, a Yale man, to honor O'Neill and establish a seminal place for theater artists in America. He had acquired a large estate on the water, that still had its cow barn standing, and it was in the barn, with the fading, painted names of the cows in the stalls, where we sat and watched Colleen Dewhurst and George C. Scott perform a scene from an O'Neill play, with José directing.

Tentative yet hopeful, in 1965 a collection of strangers came together. We sat in front of a rude platform under the estate's huge beech trees and received the blessing of the state's historian, an old professor in carpet slippers and string tie. He told us of the late-seventeenth-century days of Connecticut farmers, that had no theater but the Sunday sermon of the minister, until the time a traveling circus from England arrived, with a lion in tow! The old professor told us of the rocky soil of Connecticut, so unyielding that a farmer could hardly put down his plow for anything but death or a Sunday sermon. Yet, when the circus came—and who knew when another would come across in a sailing ship? —the farmer did stop his work, grabbed his children by the hand, and took them to see the lion. The lion was pure theater, art, the excitement of seeing what one had never seen before. The old professor squinted in the sun and looked out at us: "It takes a lot of work to make a little leisure, and a lot of leisure to make a little art, and a lot of art to make a little culture. You playwrights out there are going to be *our* lions in this century."

The challenge was there. No one sitting on the grass took it otherwise. There was young Lanford Wilson; young John Guare; young Israel Horovitz and Paul Foster; young Herb Lieberman, who became a novelist. Young Sam Shepard had departed the day before. It was all too New England and bourgeois for this lank and rumpled Wild West loner. Sam didn't need an establishment conference of bumbling peers, and he was heard to say: "This is bullshit!" Perhaps he was right about himself, but for others, the O'Neill oasis proved to be mother's milk for years to come, and a place where many plays got their obstetrical slap on the behind before going on to be acclaimed on Broadway or win Pulitzer prizes. The young writers sitting there were to become, definitely, lions of a sort, if not an Arthur Miller or a Tennessee Williams; the old professor's prophecy was realized.

It was there that even I, a composer, had to write a play. Watching the O'Neill amphitheater being built, I was seized with the desire to write something to be born in it, a play about a boy living in a small Yankee town, who wanted to be a trapeze artist, but in 1928 that couldn't happen unless you were queer or foreign, so Moxie Malone ran away to join a circus and became nothing more than a flagpole sitter, but the greatest one in the world. Of course there was music in my play, ballet, surreal dream, as at the age of fifty-seven Moxie tries to break his record by sitting up with the birds for a year. A childhood friend, Charlie Phipps, comes to see him after a lifetime, bringing boyhood love, tales, and the smell of home. Charlie, a shoe store owner, a little man who knows only the excitement of his backyard garden, the unusualness of selling a size thirteen shoe, the angst of living with a wife who has no dream . . . *does* understand Moxie's need to reach for the stars, to be an artist, the best, if only on a flagpole, though the experience strains Charlie to the point of heart attack. Catharsis comes when he helps Moxie forgive the unforgiving family and past he had left. In the kooky, rundown atmosphere of an amusement park, the two men relive, define, renew love.

The play received an enthusiastic reading in the barn the next year, two months after my father died. How he would have enjoyed knowing I could write words as well as music.

Though I was still writing music, words began to take over. A mutation, a new animal was emerging; anything could happen. I could do anything, feel anything, become something I had never been—a writer, even a betrayer.

The next summer there I was, with Willow and a new one-act play, *The Drums Make Me Nervous,* for bongo drums, flute, and tenor sax. James Hammerstein was to stage the reading, but soon discovered that my real-surreal experiment with words,

dance, music, could not be read, but had to
be realized fully if we were to learn anything
from the doing. Everyone knew I couldn't
have written the play if it hadn't happened
to me—black-and-white love. Whisper,
whisper in Connecticut. The play had also
brought the first American black actor into
the repertory of the O'Neill conference—
that fact for no reason except that no sub-
mitted play thus far had called for a black
actor. The actor arrived, sinfully handsome,
talented, ill-at-ease, and either on drugs or
drying out, we couldn't tell which. The play
perched on his head and rolled like a ball
about to fall; it required the bravura of a
man who knew who he was, despite the
world's damnation. Discomfort was everywhere for me, because of the theme of the
play as well as its experiment with music and
dance, which would have been enough to
send any actor back to ingesting cocaine.
The play fell on its face. Would it have
played better in German, my bitter-suite fan-
tasia of idealized love at first sight, killed in
the sewer of drugged streets? The play was
about racism and a sleeping white world.

It was a painful summer. What had I

done? Willow wouldn't talk to me, Jules was far away.

How far, I had no idea until I arrived in New York to an apartment shrouded in sheets and life suspended in the hot, late August twilight, an apartment too quiet, as if there had been a death. Chuck was not due back from camp yet. Then the phone rang. It was Jules. He wouldn't be home as expected, he said; he was going to make a side trip to Washington, D.C.

That was not like him. Washington had not been on the schedule, and he was vague about why he was going there now. I smelled danger in Washington. As estranged as we were, we always knew where and why each of us would be (for Chuck's sake, *his* nest, if not ours).

A suddenly exhumed Delphic oracle seized me by the scruff of the neck: "You have broken something, and the energies that create peace have been lost to the dark. You are now in a void and are led by the negative forces of void. Hence you do not exist as a wife, a mother, a woman. The years spent being those are now blank. You have destroyed your private temple. You are nothing."

I went crazy. My intuitions, suspicions, and terror were the kind that make the mouth dry, the heartbeats skip—Greek tragedy squared. I called Jules back in Colorado. "Please come home!"

"Are you sure?" Each word was slowly paced, like the steps of coffin bearers or ushers down a wedding aisle.

"Yes."

His pause, his thinking on the phone, told me how close I was to losing him. We both knew what we were talking about, without words.

"All right, I'll cancel Washington," he said. "But it won't be easy. This has to do with more than you and me."

He didn't have to tell me. There was someone who would be hurt in Washington, by what we would decide. When I hung up, I flushed with anger. *Someone.* Who in hell gave her the right to think she could take possession of what was mine, so fast! Jules?

Oh, what a bitch you are, I castigated myself. Did you think you could hurt him and not expect he would protect himself somehow? Did you think you could be as *naughty* (oh, that old word) as you wished, and he would stand by like a father?

Only later did I learn how crucial his side trip to the hot capital in August might have been, how it could have changed our personal history forever, because Jules thought he had lost me.

Was it easier to love at the edge of the Aegean, under a blue and ancient sky stuffed with gods listening? There was no noble banishment, no boat with sail to carry me, with my bruises, limps, and wounds, to distant lands where a soul may roam quite unknown. . . . I had only the brick and treeless street, no other place to hide, and just an exhumed oracle to share in my almost marriagecide. What a glassy void of a universe, without immortal Imps ready with advice, to remind me *they* throw the dice, and the fault is not all my own.

Chuck knew something bad had happened, but he trusted us. A teenager senses but prefers to ignore the fact that a world is about to crumble, until divorce hits him like a wet towel. Now, even if his family had *not* collapsed, we owed him an explanation for why life had had such strange comings and goings for a year. We tried to explain that grown-ups have a tough time figuring out things, too; it never stops—the finding out. But most important, he was loved. And there was repairing to do, not for him, but for us. Sometimes a house needs renovating, the smell of new wood, new rooms in the heart, unimagined until one begins the work. One rebuilds because the structure deserves a renewing. Would he be patient with us?

And for us? We have other "miles to walk." We had to get over a past year of: Why do you slide into nervous rest beside me, with silence your only gift? How are we to swallow this time we taste, slippery as a dead herring?

And yet another mile of: Reinforce the stitch that ties us, and I will do the same for you. Benedict this bed and I'll confess to anything.

VERMONT

Yorkers Arrive

NO MORE Fire Island for us. By 1972 it had become an upper-class Coney Island. Anyway, I, for one, had began to feel *the sea* too impersonal, vast, detached—if you weren't a sailor or a fisherman. Beach-sitting I knew too well, the cosmic roll, the seabird flight, the randomness of seaweed, driftwood, and broken shell; white-capped waves to fizzled calm; and no shade cap-a-pie.

I would always love the sea, but now I needed corners, the smell of green, the flowering of trees, the intimacy of a country road, a brook, a pond.

We had begun to dream of owning a house

snuggled into a rise of land, to feel a town square, a church steeple somewhere near. I needed the hum of growing things, big things like forests and mountains.

We decided to experiment with a dirt road, in a log cabin, from May to September. A friend of ours owned the spread of land. The small, two-floor cabin overlooked a pond; beyond the pond was a stream, and across the stream, a primeval fir forest of Vermont. Above, "up the road a way" you could hear the hum of Stratton Mountain.

We had visited our friend a number of times, leaving Willow at home with a sitter —the wrench from her routine, just for a weekend, wasn't worth the tumult. But her fur would bristle with stimulation when we returned with the smell of fir, loam, leaves, country closets.

"Come up and try it, rent my cabin, not for a weekend but a fat stretch; I mean, really live here," Malvine challenged. She had migrated to Vermont after her divorce years before, and had literally homesteaded, with her two young sons, in the log cabin at the bottom of Stratton Mountain. A strong-minded, large-boned woman, Malvine had a

firm-lipped energy and spiritual handsomeness about her that we often thought the
women of the covered-wagon days must
have had to have survived their trek into wilderness, with nothing to sustain them but
their belief in their woman-selves, their families. After a time she had built herself a
proper house across the lawn, but I think she
always viewed the cabin with a mix of rue
and pride, as evidence of her lonely bravery
and freedom from a marriage that had
failed.

Late April in Vermont there was still snow
on the ground and frost on the windows in
the morning, though crocuses were pushing
through the melting snow, and the sun was
warm enough to deck-chair in by noon. We
had moved into the cabin, rude, cozy, and
cramped as a barnacled old tugboat, with
just its fireplace as a source of heat. It could
have been the mid-eighteenth-century home-
stead of one of Ethan Allen's Green Mountain Boys, and pretty fine, at that. Considering the nerve and man-wit it had taken to
hew out a dream—a cabin in the wilderness
—it was a veritable castle.

It's not hard to feel the history of *some* landscapes and hearts as ever present, if you just close your eyes, particularly if you're outside a log cabin in Vermont. Yes, it was a veritable castle, considering . . .

The French and Indian Wars are over! England is the victor. It is the end of France's dream of domination of North America. Young American soldiers conscripted to help the British (since they were the King's subjects, too) are returning home from Canada, to their towns in Massachusetts, Connecticut, Rhode Island, to pick up their lives again as farmers, artisans, shopkeepers, or traders, to continue what their fathers and grandfathers had stunningly turned into a thriving *New* England in the short historical space of a hundred years.

The demobilized young veterans, relieved to be out from under the yoke of the pompous British military, are a band of happy men as they trek down from Canada, while waiting at home are parents, wives, and sweethearts, wondering if they were alive or dead. But the young men prolong their *vacation* as they tramp through northern territory never seen by white colonists before. *Vert mont,* the French called it. What wonders! A place of plenty, untouched beauty, rivers and lakes bursting with fish, primeval hardwood forests overflowing with game—a paradise fit for kings; and no unfriendly Indians to mar the journey, only pleasant, mild Abnakis passing through to fish and hunt.

Some of this new breed—the literate, restless, and independent grandsons of the Eastern Seaboard colonists—swore they would return to make it theirs. Americans; those always to be drunk with the limitless possibilities beyond the horizon.

"Go a little West, young man!" brought them back in trickles, then in waves, those who'd had a taste of wilderness and preferred it to the overcrowded towns and cities, with their strictures and the Calvinism of their Puritan days dying hard but slowly. (Little did they know what *overcrowded* could mean, in the future!)

They were a self-confident lot, these first Vermonters—they'd had a taste of war, knew their mettle, preferred stomping quadrilles to waltzes, wilderness and freedom to stuffy English parlors; and no one was going to tell them they couldn't hard-drink a night away after wrestling with a tree trunk to make a cabin. Yet they were still their fathers' sons—industrious, God-fearing dreamers. Thus came the Vermont spirit, the personal and political passions that were unique even for the colonies they'd left.

The young Vermont homesteaders were soon to discover that their enemy was not relentless nature or the Indian but rather the greed and venom of their own kind. The settlers had bought their land grants fair and square, from the King's Governor sitting in New Hampshire, His Excellency Benning Wentworth, a man of fancy, English gentry ways who controlled the right to sell land grants for the King's Council in London. Wentworth received a cut from all land he granted for settling. Wentworth was greedy. And who would know, in the wilderness west of him, whether he sold the same land twice over, once to the settlers and twice to absentee New Yorkers who considered the territory called Vermont part of *their* colony?

The absentee Yorkers found out and got mad. The homesteaders got even madder.

Imagine, one fine day a pouter pigeon of a man dressed in satins comes riding up on a fine horse and says: "Get off my land, squatter, this land is mine!"

"Hell, no!" you say. "It's mine! The King's Governor and you be damned! This land is Vermont and bought fair. It's not New York's or New Hampshire's, so get yourself off, or you just might have to hang from a tree by your heels for a couple of days, to think it over. By God, we don't kill anything but what to eat, yet there might come a time when we won't think twice about it!"

By 1766, New York, representing itself and the King, told all holders of "illegal" land to pay for it again or leave. (Governor Wentworth stood to make a bundle!) The next year a petition from six hundred Vermont settlers went to London to plead with the King. Nothing got settled. Sharp Yorker lawyers, armed with titles real and unreal, were throwing farmers off their land. Soon farms were being burned to the ground because the farmers wouldn't budge.

The Revolution had started. In Vermont, ten years early. Free men's rights were being assaulted! The Vermonters had to organize an army, and an army needed a general.

Ethan Allen, a giant of a man, had appeared out of Connecticut. Boisterous and contentious, he was a man of unusual passions, faults, intellect, and humanity; they had found their general. He represented them at the land title trials in Albany, presided over by a judge who was also a Yorker titleholder of disputed land. It was obvious that the favorite colony of the Crown—New York and its Tories—was going to make sure that it owned the territory known as Vermont. The Wentworth land grants to the settlers were not allowed into court as admissible evidence. The farmers lost.

At Catamount Tavern in Bennington, a meeting was called of perhaps a hundred men, who announced their plan to uphold their rights, with force if necessary. An army in buckskins would oppose the Crown!

Legends about Ethan Allen and his Green Mountain Boys began to cascade out of the mountains, down into the new towns and valleys. Allen could strangle a bear with his hands; he could outrun deer, fell an ox with a single blow. He was known to hold two New York sheriffs over his head and beat them together like frying pans until they cried out for mercy.

Many of the tales were true. Allen was six-feet-four or -five and had the breadth of a Paul Bunyan. Unhappily married, Allen was always leaving his home in Connecticut to romp through wilderness rather than drown in petty domesticity and the company of "God-fearing" hypocrites. He would leave a wake of righteous brawls wherever he went —he *had* to, self-made intellectual of the Enlightenment (New World style) that he was. He was consumed with what he called "matters of the mind," and possessed the physical strength to back it up. To be the center of a fight for free thought and dignity was his favorite use of time. The Vermont rebels couldn't have dreamed up a better pugilist-philosopher leader.

Allen wasn't the only larger-than-life man in the struggle of the Vermont farmers. There was Allen's younger cousin Remember Baker. Freckle-faced, sandy-haired, and not very tall, he seemed more boy than man, but Remember Baker, it was said, had the strength of a catamount. His friends claimed that if he were to be cut up in two, he'd most surely grow back together again. Baker had been one of those young men tramping down from Canada after the war against the French. He went home to Connecticut, got his young wife, Desire, and his baby son, and headed back to the wilderness—Arlington, Vermont.

And there was Seth Warner, who was organizing the farmers long before Allen arrived on the scene. Seth was another tall one, six-feet-two, "straight as a hickory" and as strong. Unassumingly, he did his work and let the others take the credit.

With such men leading them, the Green Mountain Boys were something to be reckoned with. From their headquarters, Catamount Tavern, they harassed, mauled, or plain humiliated the encroaching Yorkers to eye-rolling distraction. They disguised themselves as Indians and scared off British militia who would stand in dumb awe of the dead-serious tricks that worked. They would capture a Yorker lawyer or supposed titleholder, tie him to a chair, hoist him to the pole at the top of Catamount Tavern, and keep him there until his shame or body functions made him plead to be let down.

Stamina was the key to Vermont. Just keeping the fiercely individualistic Vermonters together was job for a titan. By 1774, the battle for Vermont was open rebellion.

John Duane, a Yorker lawyer the Vermonters called "swivel eye," placed a bounty on Ethan Allen's head, for his capture. Allen turned about and did the same on Duane's, saying, "The gods of the hills are not the gods of the valley. Come to Bennington if you don't know what I mean!"

The Green Mountain Boys were a staying operation. The Vermont farmers would have lost the battle but for the other drums of freedom sounding—the Revolution of *all* the colonies. It would save Vermont, at last, from being swallowed up by New York, which was the intention of the King and his "swivel-eyed" Tory collaborators.

It's no wonder, the built-in wariness of the Vermont spirit, egalitarian yet conservative-in-its-own-behalf. Yorkers aside, the other colonies weren't too interested in whether

Vermont ended up a state or not. Ethan Allen confronted George Washington himself during the Continental Congress, threatening that Vermont would become a country of its own, or God forbid, an ally of the King (he quickly thought better of that) if Vermont was not to become its own state in the Union.

As it turned out, Vermont played the reluctant bride and didn't join the Union until quite a few years after the Revolution. So much for the stubbornness of those who call the Green Mountains and forests their own.

Driving up from Manhattan, we Yorkers and a cat, we pass through Bennington, toward Manchester, with the mountains looming all around, the small, isolated towns showing their white clapboard church spires and general stores, all neat and peaceful in the late spring sun. Stubborn-chinned Vermont greeted us with one word—"ay-yuh"—and looked away. It didn't cotton much to strangers, but it didn't say "Go away" either, if you meant well. After all, wasn't Vermont *different*? Hadn't it sustained the odd, the wild, the free, the philosophical and emancipated, from the beginning?

Just remember where you are, that's all—a place of fair reason, and mind your own.

In the Garden

She wondered why I chose to go outside in
Vermont, to leave the prison of being a
house cat, unlike on that horrible Fire
Island. Two reasons: I found the
countryside to my liking; and She could
never know about the things I can notice,
observe, and hear, that she couldn't in a
million years. Maybe if she should be a cat
someday, who knows?

There was a garden in Vermont. When
she wasn't writing, She was gardening,
pruning, cutting, all that sort of thing. She
loves to garden, as did her mother and
father, it seems. Her mother grew irises;

her father liked to fuss with roses and
bushes called bridal wreath and cluck over
his umbrella tree. When her parents were
gardening, they were more pleasant to be
with. "Touched by some mysterious happy
state," She said.

I began to like crouching in the garden
because it was always full of noisy drama
that a human couldn't possibly hear. In
Vermont I even got over my aversion to
dirt. I could lie in the garden for hours,
deciding it wasn't dirty at all, but sweet-
smelling and cool.

I think it was a day in June when, all at
once, the garden rocked with screams. The
old apple tree, hard of hearing, bent down
to pick up the shrill flower sounds of
panic. A bee was tearing the petals off a
rose, one by one, stripped it bare, down to
its poor naked stem, and leaving trails of
red all around. One petal fell on my back,
but I didn't move, I wanted to see what
would happen next. The torturer flew away
fast without a sound. Little dahlias gossip a
lot. They fancy themselves as pretty as the
rose, you know, presumptuous creatures,
and if something untoward happens to a

rose, the dahlias are so pleased. One of
them, in a high little voice, commented on
what had just happened, with that nasty,
high-pitched tone of a gossip trying to be a
philosopher. "You know, of course, what
happened," said the dahlia. "It's not for
me to say about the ways of others, but
. . . that bee was spurned, that's what
happened! He came to feast on his picked
beloved, but she had given her honey to
another bee just an hour before. He was
furious, as you all can see. What ridiculous
behavior, as if she were the only flower in
the garden!"

The old apple tree threw his head back,
straightened up, and laughed. "Oh, my
aching back. . . . A moral for roses: A bee
spurned is worse than a worm turned, so
promise nothing like fidelity to a bee.
Moral for bees: Never pin your hopes on
one rose. The summer's too short for true
love. Moral for all you others: Some things
only happen to bees and roses."

When I meowed for Her to open the
cabin door to let me in, for my siesta on
the table overlooking the pond (that's what
I liked about Vermont, for the first time in

my cat life I could come and go, it was wonderful), She said, as she always did, "What have you been up to, little one?" How could I possibly tell her? If I could, she'd probably be jealous (if she believed me) that there are some doings in life you can observe only if you are a cat. That thought deepened my purr with satisfaction as I fell off to sleep on the table facing the pond.

Out of the Forest

MUCH to our surprise, Willow took to Vermont; not like a duck to water—her reactions were too keen for that. More like a Bernard Berensen drinking in the work of one of his favorite Renaissance painters. Ah, the country air for a neurasthenic. A wonderful place to think and write. All her responses were contrary to what we had expected. She loved the cramped quarters of the cabin, the natural smells of untreated wood, the seducing odors of the forest coming in the windows, and the spring sun. Lying on a dining-room table anywhere was forbidden (no rear ends where plates go, madam!), but the large, handmade table in the windows facing the pond was so irresistible, with the sun turning the satiny wood into a gleaming bed soft as fur the color of maple syrup . . . how could one say no to that? Particularly when you knew that field mice used it as a playing field at night; then why not a cat during the day?

Willow began to take daily constitutionals. She looked like a miniature Lippizaner, her tiny paws prancing high in the tall grass, so as not to get her fur too belly-close to the spring wetness.

She would emerge every day, parasol in hand, in case; fill her lungs with the elixir of pine, look up at the sky, and turn her head back and forth in wonderment for the clouds. *From a cat's-eye view, clouds can be incredible.* If someone were with her, she would turn to share her pleasure, catch their eyes with hers. Down across the banks of the pond she went, sniffing at the new clover, Indian paint, wild thyme; then down to the stream, where she would stand for ages, peering into the mysteries of the forest on the other side, leaning her head to the right, the left, trying to see what lay beyond the huge, first-growth tree trunks. What went on in there? What could come out and take one by surprise, or fill one with terror? The energetic flashing in the kink of her tail told all her thoughts.

It was not her nature to scramble over the rocks in the narrow part of the stream, to get to the other side like a silly chicken.

But *something* would come out of the forest one day; she just knew it. Her daily walk always ended with a swinging-tail, vigilant peering into the woods.

One day it happened. The sky fell in, for Willow, in Vermont.

A kitten came. A brown, scruffy, black-striped little tiger with green eyes—no older than Willow was when we found her in the garbage can.

He came catapulting through the pinecone-strewn forest floor on the other side of the stream, like a little warrior on horseback. Oh, he made it known that he was resourceful and terribly clever about life in the woods; he wanted no sympathy. But it was obvious that much was bravado—he was too young for such a life.

He had a hacking cough and a festering sore on the tip of his chin. We presumed the sore was from peeking down a gopher hole once too often. And he suffered from a debilitating dysentery that sent him screaming with abdominal pains back into the wood— his litter box *nonpareil*. We deduced *that* by following him after one of his screams, and proved it to ourselves, with Willow watching from the *safe* side of the stream that we had jumped, not as nimbly as the little tiger, who had every dry rock figured out to perfection. We saw him relieve himself of sick brown water instead of healthy stool, but the little thing would recover almost immediately, to what, clear to anyone, was an ingratiating spirit filled with the joy of life, sick brown water notwithstanding.

He would arrive! He would leave! The following days were filled with pure theater— Feydeau, Molière, commedia dell'arte. From what door-of-a-tree would he make his entrance? What new scene would he play in front of the cabin, with a bird in mouth, almost as big as he? What snake or chipmunk would he corner? But he always left screaming, back into the woods with that abdominal pain intruding on his adventurous, playful days. We figured he had to be a magnificent hunter to be able to sustain himself in the winter-turned-spring. A born little survivor.

We named him Killer Kelly. A feisty Irishman he was, a snub-nosed Jimmy Cagney, all swagger and heart.

Willow called him "the little bastard." She would have none of him, and when Kelly began to show Jules his pine forest, on long walks together—"like a little dog, you wouldn't believe it," Jules reported—Willow took to the cabin to protect her turf and wouldn't come out. We respected her wishes, but what happened outside was beyond her control and ours. Jules would be sunning in the deck chair and suddenly Kelly would materialize, jump up on Jules, wrap himself around his neck, and go to sleep, with an asthmatic purr as loud as a swarm of bees in a honeysuckle bush.

We were of two minds: We had to get that kitten to a vet. No, we shouldn't; we don't need another cat, either in the cabin or the New York apartment. But his chin was festering and he seemed to be getting thinner. If we had wanted to scoop him up, Kelly wasn't making it easy. He made himself un-catchable; even curled around Jules's neck, if he *sensed* hands reaching out to grab him, he jumped away like a spark. Yet he seemed to want *in* with us, but only on his terms. He was doing it in wide circles—it was a matter of pride, after all. You didn't go and collapse on someone's doorstep.

In—with her family, her cabin? Willow was outraged with us for even entertaining the thought. But Kelly's wide circles of pride were getting smaller and closer to the cabin. He was no fool—he knew he would lose his battle for survival in the pine forest if he didn't make it into that cabin for a hot meal and shelter, if he couldn't stir (not again!) our feeling of cosmic responsibility.

We began to feel nasty and ugly, and what's more, fed up with Willow's outrage. Kelly's trust was growing; he took to sitting on the porch, and the battle of the screen door began. He would press his nose against the screen, trying to read our minds. Would they? Wouldn't they? On the other side of the screen sat Willow, growling, banging her little paws against the screen to make him go away. "Away with you, nasty, evil-smelling infidel!" She was right; poor Kelly did smell from the sickness in his bowels—a desperate hunter didn't have the time or inclination to wash himself.

He still wouldn't let us catch him. Playing by his rules meant he would get *in* by conquering the cabin. Kelly figured it all out— how to invade, and not through the front door. It happened when the weather had turned winter again one evening. Inside was a fireplace and a pot of stew on the stove. He scrambled up the apple tree leaning over the cabin, jumped onto the roof, pushed a dormer screen in, and there he was, downstairs, smiling. Out you go! Scramble! Hiss! Willow almost had a heart attack. Our guilt was reaching the point of flagellation as the only redemption. Fortunately, the weather went back to spring the next day, but Kelly found a plate of food for him on the porch. All right, we'd have two cats for the summer, one inside and one out. The porch became Kelly's when he wasn't hunting. He was eating porch *and* forest food; he was as wary as we, and wasn't going to lose his hunting prowess in case we withdrew our charity.

His little belly began to get fat with forest food and cat food in it every day.

The screen door battle changed character. No more hissing and slapping. One nose was on the outside, the other was in. More often than not, the noses found themselves pressing against each other.

After a while, if he wasn't on the porch, Willow furtively peered out the screen, looking for him. It seems one can get used to anything, even miss it when it's not there.

After a while, all right, if there's food on the porch all the time, he'd accept a bell around his neck to warn the birds. The first time we called Kelly by name, he knew he was winning. We had earned his trust. His walks with Jules became a daily ritual.

At night he slept against the chimney. That bothered me terribly. I blew my stack, and in front of Willow. "I will not have that little creature up there alone at night! It isn't fair! He deserves better, damn it, and if the selfish ones around here don't like it, let them go up there and sleep in the cold, damp night and see if they could take it so courageously and with such dignity! So watch out, everyone! I'm opening up that screen door for Kelly tomorrow!"

"Are you serious?" Jules said. "Two cats?"

"Absolutely."

"I agree. You know, the first thing we have to do is take him to a doctor, but I think he'll let us now."

Willow saw it coming. She had been out-voted.

The next day Kelly marched in with no grin of victory, just a soft brrp of thank you, slowly removed his knight's armor, laid down his sword and shield against the fox, the raccoon, all the terrors for a kitten in the wilderness, and collapsed in front of the fire-place.

"The little bastard," she mumbled, going over to sniff him a begrudging welcome, per-haps not without admiration for his pluck. My yelling had hit a nerve—the memory of her own struggle to keep alive in that dread-ful tenement cellar next to the boiler. Fate had ruined her summer again, but that was life—the baffling Hand of the Absolute.

Once the little thing let his guard down, we had a very ill cat on our hands. The country vet couldn't seem to cure his dysentery, but Kelly got stronger with regular food and managed to maintain himself. He was all cat, still spending most of his days outside, pouncing, hunting, but not eating his catch; at night he would come in for dinner, then smell up Willow's immaculate pan with his persistent diarrhea.

Willow's summer was spent being of two minds. She was in a state of exhaustion, either hating or being intrigued by Kelly. Those who become the butt of our beastly behavior show us the worst in ourselves, and we don't like them for it. She hated herself and hated Kelly for it. She took long naps on Baudelaire's *Flowers of Evil* and actually threw up one day all over Camus' *The Plague*. On the other hand, we caught the two of them actually taking a walk together along the bank of the pond, right up to the stream. Kelly jumped across and waited for her on the other side, but Willow turned back—no forest play for her.

Elizabeth joined us for a few weeks in the cabin. "Who's this?" she said, looking down at the gangling little tiger lying in the hearth. "Another cat? When did that happen?"

"Don't ask," I said, and proceeded to tell her Kelly's tale, as far as we knew it.

Elizabeth slept in one of the tiny bedrooms on the second floor, the one where Kelly used to push in the screen after climbing up the apple tree. He took to doing it again, to surprise her and play games; she would find him wrapped around her neck and purring when she woke in the morning. "What an enchanting little boy." She took over the endless poulticing of the sore he still had on his chin. Three times a day he would hold up his little face, allowing the hot soaks with a face cloth and then the antibiotic cream. In her persistent, methodical way, Elizabeth cured that end of him, but nothing was helping the dysentery. Even so, his patient, gentle nature was emerging by the day; it was impossible not to love him.

Would we take him home with us or wouldn't we, she wanted to know. We'd try to find someone to take him in, in Vermont, *maybe,* we said we were thinking. "You *must* take him with you," Elizabeth pronounced, her cool, green-blue eyes disapproving. "He needs a New York vet, the best without question." She was smitten with Kelly.

"Why don't *you* take him?"

With her elegant "Don't be silly," the subject was closed; it was our problem.

However, Elizabeth took on the challenge of Willow's hurt feelings, and the two of them spent much time together, combing their hair, doing their nails, whispering, and being "ladies." It was clever of Elizabeth to know how much Willow needed that kind of thing.

Abduction

IT WAS late August. A decision had to be made about Kelly. We decided to visit the farmer a mile or so up the road and ask him if he'd noticed a little brown tiger cat this summer that had been roaming about. "We've been feeding it ever since late May," we said, "but we're going back to the city after Labor Day. Could you take him in? He's a people cat now; it would be a shame if—" The old man interrupted with a pleasant snort:

"That little thing? I wondered what happened to him! He was around here since early April. Smart little tyke. Figured out, every chimney that had smoke coming out of it would feed him, and then he'd run off, scared of the big cats in the barn, I guess. He's still alive? Well, well . . . thought he didn't make it. Good for him. Sure we'll take him, but don't know whether he'll like it. The other cats don't like strangers much. They can get pretty ornery about it; he might end up in the woods again."

The old man, looking like a creased, weathered pine himself, sized us Yorkers up; he knew us only by sight, from our walks along the road and a summer of friendly waves. He began to laugh. "You know how that little thing got up here? He ain't no Vermont cat. Funniest damn thing you ever heard. Come in an' have some coffee."

And this is what he told us:

"Right after a big snow, early April—it sure does come on us, confusin' the hell outta the buds—I'm down at the mailbox, an' this man with a beard is gettin' outta his beat-up station wagon, an' he's holdin' a kitten. Damned if he didn't put the little thing down in the snow, and off it ran. Weird-lookin' he was—the man, not the cat. You city people see lots of them, you know what I mean.

"I said: 'What did you just do? Your cat's gonna get lost.' An' I also said: 'Or are you dumpin' it?' I didn't like the look of him. The back of his car was all filled with junk, pieces of rusty iron or something, you never saw such a mess as in that car.

"Nosy me, I said: 'You're not plannin' to dump the junk around here, are ya? That ain't allowed.'

"He looked at me like I was dumb or something, an' he said he was a sculptor an' the junk wasn't junk, though it might look like it. An' he was in a hurry, he said, on his way back to New York; he'd driven all the way up just to drop off the cat.

"I said, 'Drop it off for what? Are you crazy? That's gonna be the end of that animal, in these here woods and snow.'

"I remember it all pretty good, 'cause I'd never heard such nonsense in my life. You know what he said? God is my witness. He said he was leavin' the cat up here, 'cause . . . it had something to do with, what was the word he said? . . . 'Zen.' That's it.

"Ever heard of it? He said he was leavin'

the kitten in the woods to find its purity, an' if God wanted him to make it, he would, an' be a special cat, all clean in his soul.

"Lord, lord, I stood there with my mouth open an' watched him take off like a bat outta hell, like somethin' was chasin' him. Damndest thing, those artist people . . . never heard such talk an' doin' in my life. Some people carry on like molasses tryin' to climb a hill in July." The old farmer banged his forehead with a fist and began to laugh. "Guess the kitten found his purity and God, all right—he found you people!"

The old man walked us out to the road, evidently with the kitten that became Kelly still on his mind, because after exchanging the usual country pleasantries about the weather, August moons, harvest, "an' before you know it, another winter," he said, "It's none of my business, but nice people like you, an' that animal survivin' like he did, you oughta take him with you an' give him a good home, if it ain't a big trouble."

Two seconds down the road, on the way back to the cabin, of course the decision had been made. Jules looked at me and said, "It's two cats back to the city, right?" I nodded my head. "Did you ever hear such an insane story? Not in a million years could he have made it up. A wacked-out Zen Buddhist sculptor, no less."

We walked on in silence. It was late afternoon and the sun had backlit the hills with an incredible amber flush. "Are you crying?" Jules asked, looking over at me.

"Yes."

"Why? What have I done now?" He laughed.

He put his arms around me in the middle of the road.

"It's Kelly. His brave little spirit. Remember how small he was in April? I can't bear thinking about it, that son of a bitch!"

It turned out to be one of the most unusual Labor Day weekends. A bearded man came up the road, walked across the lawn, and came up to us sitting on the bank of the pond. "Hi," he said. "I've just come from the farmer up the road. I'm looking for my cat. He says you people in the cabin might know where he is."

Jules stood up. I said, "You what?"

"A brown cat with black markings? Like a tiger?" Jules asked.

"Yes, that's the one."

Between Jules and me, I can't remember who said what, but it went something like this:

"When did you last see him?"

"Four months ago. I left him off, up the road," the sculptor said. (Of course it was the wacked-out one. Who else could it be?)

"You're looking for *your* cat? He's *our* cat now!"

"I beg your pardon?" the man said.

"You heard me. You abandoned him in the woods!"

"I didn't abandon him, I gave him the opportunity to undergo a rigorous religious test." It was said with a sly humility, someone who was talking to people on a plane beneath him, and he was being patient with their ignorance. He actually extended his hand and introduced himself quite civilly, as if he had no idea he was facing two people black with anger. Chuck had come back from his summer in camp and was sitting there with us on the bank. The air didn't have a healthy feel to it, so Jules suggested

Chuck go for a swim and we'd take our "guest" back to the cabin.

Willow followed us in. Kelly, thank goodness, wasn't around.

Once inside, we let him talk about what he had done with this kitten who had been born in his loft in the West Village, how it was the runt of the litter and had been funny and sick, so he had decided to make a spiritual experiment. All spirits, whether human or animal, must confront the Great One. He had prayed the kitten would make it, he said, but in the final analysis it wasn't his prayers but the individual's karma that would effect a miracle, if a miracle were destined, and evidently it was, and here he was, to retrieve his cat.

It would have been very funny if it hadn't turned nasty.

"He is *not* your cat, he's ours. We've taken care of him, brought him to a doctor, named him. You abandoned him and he would have died if not for us. You're four months late. Finders keepers, losers weepers," I expelled, in as controlled a tone as I could manage.

"The hell you say!" He was losing his Zen cool by the minute.

There we were, three grown-up people. Maybe this man was a fine sculptor. Who knew? He certainly had the look of the *committed:* pale, rice-diet thin; piercing eyes, naked cheeks, distracted hair and clothing . . . he could be a genius for all we knew, but a crazy one, obviously, when it came to cats and the cosmos.

Jules and I, without even eye orders to each other, were rowing together like expert punters. Give him his space, keep it soft. We changed the subject and talked of other things like "cabbages and kings."

We offered him some wine, we talked more about how "the sea is boiling hot, and whether pigs have wings." Until we ran out of subjects and it had to come back to Kelly. The sculptor expressed amusement over the name. We told him dear stories about the cat's maneuvers around, around, until he had wound himself about our cabin and hearts; his bravery, his this, his that. . . . The idea that it would be unfair to take Kelly away from us wasn't getting through, because he followed our confiding sentiment with:

"Incidentally, where is he? I'll take him

with me now. My car is parked on the side of the road up near that farmer's spread. I'm sleeping in it tonight and plan to take off tomorrow around noon."

"You can't take him, he's not around, he's in the woods," Jules said.

"You're not going to take him, he's ours," I said.

There ensued a violent discussion about the definition of ownership in the Universe, with long words and in loud tones. It got pretty wild, and Willow sat on the dining-room table, enthralled, making believe she was washing her tail. She'd lick and lift her head up, turn back to lick, then stop again to listen. She was beside herself, I knew it, and I couldn't help a silent laugh. Half of her wanted the sculptor to win, and half of her was disgusted with him. Such divided emotion caused her to be overcome by alternating fits of sneezing and yawning. She was glued to the scene and understanding its every turn.

Chuck's swim had long been finished, but he was smart enough not to come in and went to visit Malvine in the big house across the lawn. She had not followed the saga of

Kelly all summer, because *at that time* she wasn't a cat person and the subject didn't interest her at all when we mentioned it. She didn't approve of the idea of house cats; country people didn't look at it the same way, she said. Cats were for barn living, and if they didn't earn their keep, that's the way the cookie crumbled. The whole idea of buying cat food in a supermarket made her snort. It wasn't natural, it was city-foolish, heedless of the cat's function: mousing. Needless to say, our friend got her comeuppance a few years later. Another little cat walked out of the woods, collapsed on *her* doorstep, made it known that this was the last stop, and stayed to become her best and trusted, pampered friend.

I heard Kelly jump up on the woodpile out on the porch. So did Willow. She got off the table, asked to go out, and we let her.

The argument inside had reached a point where the sculptor said: "Where is he? I'm going out to find him, and if I don't, I'm coming back tomorrow morning."

We went out to the porch. Willow was sitting on the edge, her back to us, and didn't turn around. Kelly was nowhere to be seen. She looked like a no-hear, no-see, no-speak toy monkey. The man walked down to the pond, as far as the stream, looked around, came back. No Kelly.

Kelly didn't appear until night, for a very late supper, his face tight with worry. He knew all about it. Willow had told him all. What was going to happen to him?

Damn the Zen-geist of a deranged sculptor! We packed that night and left early the next morning, a week before we had planned to leave.

We kidnapped Kelly, plain and simple, and didn't even tell our friend across the way that we were leaving. She would have thought us mad.

Poor little Kelly. Whisk! Into the car where he'd never been. Gone the pine forest, the apple trees, the cozy cabin. The little nature boy shivered and cowered in Jules's arms, sitting in the backseat. Willow sat up front in Chuck's lap, staring at the white lines of the road, but letting out a meow every now and then—a not usual thing for her to do. I think, as much as she might have been thinking: What a revolution Vermont turned out to be! Two cats going back to the apartment. Democracy! It's the end of my monarchy. . . . she was also trying to comfort Kelly in the back with her intermittent meow. Because poor Kelly, torn between fear and trust, even if he *was* in Jules's lap, had been wrenched from the only reality he could remember, and he couldn't stop crying.

Chuck considered the whole thing a gas. His parents were abductors; we were all fleeing away before dawn! Pretty soon we'd hear police sirens and the sculptor in hot pursuit. What fun! But it was Chuck who had already begun to think practically:

"We're gonna need another cat's pan," he sang out. "Where are we gonna put it? Not in my room . . ."

The little warrior of the pine forest was so frightened his first night in the city, he crawled under the heavy Victorian couch. I cried because, of all the places to hide in the apartment, he had chosen the protection of my father's couch, the white elephant that had sat in the parlor when I was growing up.

I had often hid behind it myself, to hate the world, then put my pieces together after I'd been punished for some crime I couldn't help repeating, born recidivist that I was, when I was small. I couldn't stand that Kelly might think our transplanting him, in one hysterical leap, from his beloved forest to a place of alien smells and sounds, the grinding of garbage trucks, fire engines screeching . . . was punishment.

Early the next morning, he crawled out and became very ill in front of our eyes, from both ends—throwing up and letting out brown water. All his defenses had left him. We brought him to the grand and famous veterinarian who prodded, listened, took X rays, stool samples, and said Kelly just might not make it. He was filled with parasites from living off wild things, he told us, and country cats rarely live long if that's their only food; he also had a severe case of asthmatic bronchitis. But he'd try to save him if he could. We told him about seeing the vet in the country, and the infection on Kelly's chin that had been cured; how come not the rest? "Sometimes they're not up on the latest," the New York doctor said kindly.

"How could Kelly have lasted the summer if he's so sick?" we asked.

"That mysterious healer, spirit," the doctor said plainly. "I should keep him here, but I'm going to let you take him home and see if we can treat him there; at least he'll be with people he's used to. And you have your other cat; that should help him."

"Well, that remains to be seen. . . . You remember the duchess, Doctor?" Jules bantered softly, the situation being too serious for a laugh.

We took Kelly home and kept him in our bedroom, with a croup kettle going day and night for the bronchitis that had turned into pneumonia, and pills around the clock for everything.

Do I wish him dead? No, I don't wish him dead. I just wish he'd go away, like a bad dream, back to Vermont on the wings of *something*, poor thing.

Kelly recovered. He made it!

Every morning for weeks after, Willow would say to him, as if she had never seen him before: "Who are *you*?"

And every morning he would answer sweetly: "I'm not sure."

A few weeks into Kelly's recovery, the phone rang. It was the sculptor. He had found our name in the phone book, he said, pleased with himself. "Yes?" I said.

He launched right into it, his voice sounding firm, yet removed, soft, as if he were *on* something: "OK, he's your cat now, I'll agree to that. . . ."

"You have no right, after what you did, to agree or disagree to anything. He's ours, and that's that. Please don't call here again," I said.

"If I find out, and I have my ways," he interjected quickly, "that you people are thinking of taking his power away, denying his sex, I'll sue you. You won't hear the end of me, I swear."

"Don't you ever call here again," I said, and hung up on him, shaking. He never did.

But a month later, we were faced with the decision: *Do* we neuter the young chieftain with eyes too clear to behold? God knows that spirit was in short supply. Would neutering him kill it? Was it fair to keep a

young male cooped up in a city apartment?
Would we let him roam the rooftops or skitter through traffic, looking for a mate? Of
course not! But he'll spray all over the furniture, in corners; it's an odor that can never
be washed away. You see, maybe we should
have left him in Vermont, to be what he was
supposed to be! Don't be ridiculous, he
would have died! (We would have lied to
deny that that damned sculptor's hubris was
not in the room.)

Back and forth it went, with Kelly's
jaunty little balls on the cutting edge.

BACK HOME

Kelly (Only a Cat)

It's obvious this creature is meant to be
only a cat. He hasn't come to ascend or
descend. He's stuck in *cat* and I'm stuck
with him.

He fawns, he runs to them when they
call. He greets them at the door. He rushes
around singing "Good morning" when he
wakes, as if he were a bird, not a cat. He's
got everything all mixed up, the little
bastard. The way he licks people's hair, sits
on their shoulders like a monkey; he eats
like a pig and makes noise like a dog when
he drinks. I've already tried to teach him a
few manners, but he's either stupid or

stubborn, I'm not sure which *yet*. But I do know this life will never be the same.

I have been trying to give him lessons. I waited until he was feeling better, the poor thing was so sick. Even I stayed up all one night wondering if he would take his last breath, his breathing was so in-and-out funny.

Pneumonia, She called it. Imagine a cat running around with pneumonia all summer and not letting anyone know about it. "Plucky," they call him? I call it dumb. Naturally, I had to wait until he got well before trying to change his ways.

It is I who learn something, not he. I learn that he is all instinct and no thinking.

He sits respectfully, seems to listen carefully, then off he goes, doing the same thing he did before. Take the litter pan, for instance.

They went out and bought a large one for the two of us to share. Wrong! We each should have our own.

The pan business is making me so nervous, I don't think I can tolerate it. Every day I have to face nausea, revulsion, not to mention anger.

I will never accept his behavior in the pan. He doesn't cover what he does, he isn't careful about going in and out, he doesn't wash himself afterward! He acts as if he were too busy for such minor details. Whoosh, he's in; whoosh, he's out, strewing the floor with litter; you'd think a sandstorm hit the room.

I mean, really: If you don't cover what your bowels let out, you foul the air, and with not a thought about anyone else. He's nothing but a little savage. They laugh and call him "nature's child." Let *them* try living with someone who never flushes *their* toilet and see how they'd feel!

The whole thing is making me so agitated, I dread using the pan—having to spend hours getting myself clean afterward. That's all we've been occupied with since we returned from Vermont, is: Kelly, Kelly, Kelly. They should worry about me—I'm a wreck.

Words, words, words.

He says: "Have you noticed that Willow spends the whole day washing herself? Has she gone bananas?"

She says: "Yes, it's O.C.S."

"O.C. what?" He says. And so did I.

"Obsessive-compulsive syndrome," She says. "A washing, hair-pulling tic. It's an old, programmed, evolutionary need. When the psyche finds itself in danger, the cogs grind into the program of self on the most fundamental level. You know, you've seen a monkey in one of those old-time zoo cages, out of its mind with being caged, and it keeps picking, picking. Or an elephant banging its trunk incessantly against a wall. . . . I remember, there was a girl in college who couldn't stop washing her hands, it was terrible. She didn't have time for anything else and had to drop out. It was so sad."

"Willow's miserable about the pan," He says.

(EUREKA! I say to myself. Maybe words will become deeds.)

"We don't have room for two pans; she'll have to make the best of it," She says. "Maybe you should try giving Kelly some lessons in hygiene, Jules. He'll listen to you, he adores you. Talk to him, cover up his little turds. He'll learn, he's so eager to please, the sweetie."

And what do you think I've been trying to do? I said to myself. If I can't teach him, no one can. He's all instinct and no brain, your little sweetie.

I must mention his other revolting habit, which maybe I could have handled if he had stayed small.

Once he recovered from all his disease, that's all he did was grow. Into a big . . . male . . . cat. Handsome, actually, even I had to admit. If he had grown up ugly, I don't know what I would have done. Probably would have tried to open a bottle of Lysol and lap it until I died. Before I knew it, he had grown to twice my size. Living close to the floor with someone twice-my-size-ugly would definitely have warranted my suicide.

He began to hide behind a door, and suddenly—pounce! there he was on my back. Trying to mount me! The concussion of his weight made me sprawl, lose my bearings totally. Oh, Absolute Peaceful Hand, not again shades of the cellar next to the boiler, not again under the damp pilings of a house on Fire Island!

I fainted every time he tried to mount me.

And what did They do? They laughed, because He said, "Kelly's trying to mount Athena."

But, thank the Absolute, off they took him to the doctor and got him "fixed." Life was bliss for the few days he was gone. When he returned, at least there was no more pouncing on my back. He was definitely changed. He didn't rush about so much, he was more attentive to my lectures about eating habits and toilet ways; but I never succeeded in making him care whether drops of milk were on his whiskers or not. To tell the truth, I didn't succeed in much of anything with him. We came to some kind of adjustment, I suppose.

You could never tell, with Kelly, whether he was listening to you or not. He would look at you with clear eyes, but he wasn't *with* you, not completely. Behind his eyes there was always the forest in them. I do believe that.

After a while we managed, he and I. Maybe there is even something about him I am jealous of. He can just *be*. He has a quiet in him, like when I saw the ocean for the first time. It just *was*. Whereas I am always moving from one state to another, exhausting myself trying to fathom the riddle of moving. He has no notion where I am most of the time, to this day.

One thing he *has* learned about me and tries to honor in his dim-witted way: no licking, no kissing, no touching. If he forgets and tries? Slap! But he has the memory of a newt. A few days go by and he forgets. It's my cross to bear—having to live side by side with someone who doesn't know how to do anything smart, except loving.

The Silver Fork

One day I was watching Her set the table for dinner. It was a real fuss for special company—the good silver, linen, a centerpiece of floating daisies, the works. She always gets nervous when guests are invited formally, two weeks in advance. It's the same kind of anxiety when she sits at the typewriter: Is it right? How does it look?

She doesn't like to be pinned down to a date, a time, a commitment. But if someone calls from the corner telephone booth and asks, "What's for dinner?" she can whip up the best cuisine you've ever tasted, and with good cheer, not a moment of that anxiety.

She was about to lay down a fork and her eyes caught mine. "Doesn't the table look romantic?"

I hear everything she says to herself; I wonder if she knows. I mean *everything.*

She sat down and lit one of her filthy cigarettes and began to stare into space.

Oh, oh . . . I thought, there she goes again, into the fog. It must have something to do with the fork. Maybe this time she'll figure it out, but I doubt it. Humans spend most of their time making fog, getting lost in it, trying to work their way out of it. I mean: they have an experience that's important. Whether it's good or bad, they cover it up with fog. Then their memory calls it up and they say, Oh, I can't go back into *that,* to figure out what happened, because I'd get lost, it's too dangerous, there's too much fog. So they never discover the truth about anything.

I ask you: Which is better, to perceive in an instant, the way I do, or to have long memory and perceive nothing?

* * *

I know that I am impatient. Cannot my
eyes see more than hers? Cannot my ears
hear more than hers? I am more beautiful,
She tells me over and over. She tells me
that, according to humans, I was an
Egyptian goddess once, goddess of fertility.
I had my own temples! They even made
me a mummy, like they did with the
pharaohs, I was that important. I know all
of that in my bones, but not in my
memory. She tells me the Romans were the
ones who brought me to Europe, and I
didn't do well there after a while. I was
considered a partner of the Devil and
demons, especially when I was the color
black; and humans stopped worshiping me;
they were afraid of me. I also know *that* in
my bones; it still makes me wary.

She tells me: In what they called the
Middle Ages, I was suddenly liked again,
because I was useful. I hunted and killed
the rats that were carrying a black plague
everywhere. My body doesn't remember
that at all. I don't think I ever hunted; that
must have been a different kind of cat! Yet
She tells me: They took me across oceans
on sailing ships, to keep them clean of rats,

and that's how I ended up, centuries later, where I did, a kitten in a cellar in New York City. The only thing I can figure is: The Absolute must be having fun with me, because the only memory I have in my body is being a goddess or being persecuted.

That's why I'm so curious about human memory, how it's used, and whether it makes you better or worse. If humans can't remember what they were, even in their bones, the way I can (except for hunting and killing!), then what good is memory?

"What now?" I meow. "Where are you going now in your endless memory, holding that fork in the air?"

I could feel Willow's eyes on me while I set the table. She was sitting on the top of the tall buffet, and that made us eye to eye. With her tail neatly curled around her front paws, she was in her Egyptian position, and her opal eyes were waiting.

"Guests are coming. I don't have time," I said.

She was not to be dissuaded. "You said,

'Doesn't the table look romantic?' And then you got one of your fuzzy looks. . . ."

"Willow!"

"I thought your memory could come back complete in a second, if you wanted it to."

"It can, it does. I was just reminded of something very romantic. *Roman,* novel of the soul, it's always romantic."

"A lesson in human?"

"What other do I have? Not a cat one; for that I defer to you, my pet."

She arched her back. "We're both doing well in lessons."

I laughed. "Jules thinks we've become two cats in one."

She thought about that for a moment. "You know, I'm fond of him, I trust him, but I love you."

"Willow, you've never said that before!"

She had flustered herself with such an avowal, and went on as if it hadn't happened. "Well, now He has Kelly for his own. But could you please tell him to do something about Kelly lying around his neck like a fur piece at the dinner table? It's unseemly."

"Unseemly? Where did you learn that?"

"You use it all the time." She went on: "Some of your guests don't like it, but they're too polite to say so, and it makes me shudder with embarrassment—a man sitting at the head of the table with a cat around his neck."

"There are some things no one can do anything about, Willow; it has to do with love, and that's that. People either understand or they don't."

She harrumped, as she usually did when it concerned Kelly.

I put the fork in its place; now everything was ready for dinner. A French daube (stew) with shallots and mushrooms, marinated out of its mind in Burgundy, cloves, peppercorns, garlic, bay leaf, and onions; a cucumber-lettuce salad in the fridge, getting itself icy and waiting for its thyme dressing, to relieve the palate of the rich hotness of the beef. . . . The decaf coffee beans had been ground (I should have waited, but I didn't, I hate the sounds of preparation, I like things to appear like magic); and dessert would be easy: orange ices, fruit, sliver-thin crackers, runny cheese for those who didn't care about dying too soon.

I did have time to go back into the fog, if I wanted to. Wasn't memory an extravagant gift to be called forth with the press of a button, or the glint of a fork lying on the table?

WORLD WAR II

I would say for me sex and the supernatural go very much together. I feel that the desire of one human being for another is not only a desire of the body but also of the soul. The two —a man and a woman, or two men, or two women—when they embrace and they say they cannot live without each other, and they fall one upon the other with a madness, that *is not just the act of flesh, it's more than flesh.*

Isaac Bashevis Singer

Perfect Love/
Perfect War

THE silver fork was like a glass paper-weight filled with scenes, even the weather of the fall of 1943. A world at war was under its dome.

Willow's chomping about no act goes unnoticed by the Absolute Peaceful Hand; her urgency to refine herself lest there be hell to pay the next time around; her quixotic, who's-to-say-it-isn't-so philosophic meows, I am amazed to say, had influenced me . . . *not* to paw through the past like a scavenger in a stranger's garbage can, but rather like a passionate curator committed to the act of

organizing—if life is art—evaluating, under-
standing the objects of my "collection."

When I was young . . .

When Russian snows were turning red,
burning flesh corrupting the air of Western
Europe . . .

When the world was caught for a brief
historical moment in the glory of Absolutes
. . . Good and Evil and no question about
it . . .

When American boys were lying split-
open-stinking in Pacific atolls; African
deserts graffitied with jagged pieces of black-
ened German and British tanks and limbs—
steel and muscle curling into rind on the relentless equatorial griddle . . .

When ships were sinking with gagging
soldiers, sailors, lungs exploding with water,
all whooshing down to the ocean bottoms,
gone forever . . .

When France had already been sold into
the white-slave trade by its own—gang-bang
raped to the tune of German drinking songs;
Italy's skin flayed strip by strip with knives
of equal betrayal, and poor Greece lying naked, invaded, shamed, its hands trying to
hide its groin, its beautiful breasts . . .

When a thousand years of European history were being bombed, dissolved into a crazy dust of stone, metal, glass, bodies, gargoyles, fonts, arches, crosses, Hebrew stars . . .

When I was in college and wore pleated, plaid skirts, knee socks, cashmere sweaters (and pearls for dress-up), otherwise, culottes, jumpers; Harris tweed overcoats and slouch hats (just like today!), I lived in a basement apartment on Christopher Street in Greenwich Village. Under the street window I had an ebony grand piano whose strings got sprayed with drops of urine occasionally when a drunk mistook my grillwork for a *pissoire.* It was a cozy one-room apartment, and I had a cat. I always had a cat and brass candlesticks wherever I lived. I cleaned the apartment once a week, and had laundry service for ironed sheets, even on my student's allowance. My dead mother's eyes commanded me always: "What can shine *must* shine." And wherever I lived was the Steinway piano that made the lowliest digs look like a castle.

I was rushing to get to Café Society, the only integrated nightclub in Manhattan—to hear Josh White, the marvelous folk and blues singer, perform. It had been rumored that he would sing his rendition of "Strange Fruit," a song about a lynching down South that could wrench your heart out of its cavity. I didn't have to rush too far. Café Society was just across little Sheridan Square Park, which my windows looked out on, and down a short block. I was rushing to meet my ex-brother-in-law, Elizabeth's first husband before she married Peter's father. Bob had known me since I was little. He and Elizabeth had been sweethearts ever since they'd met in a summer camp, the one Elizabeth went to when I was busy screaming in the forest and drowning at Camp Don't Worry. They had married too young and were too selfish, still clay to be formed. I had known him all my life; he was family, whether divorced or not. And Bob loved music. He could whistle whole concerti and Bach's entire B Minor Mass, as well as any digging, driving jazz riff you could want.

The divorce was new and Bob was footloose. "Are you studying? Josh is singing tonight. Want to meet me? I'll get there first and get a table close to the piano."

There was no street fear in those days. The streets were your second living room. A girl in a pleated, plaid skirt could go anywhere by herself, even to a nightclub. Days of innocence at home mixed with days of true evil abroad. The air crackled with everything larger than life in the perfect war. Soldiers were everywhere, and death was in the newspapers every day. We weren't winning the war. That was a strange concept for Americans—not winning. It was very scary, even inconceivable, yet you went to school, did what you were supposed to do. The war had not touched me personally, except for "my love." Deferred from active duty because he was in medical school, he nonetheless wore a uniform several times a month for meetings of the National Guard, and he always seemed different when he wore it— the uniform meant he might have to leave at any moment.

But I was used to that, his leaving at any moment. It had more to do with his character than the uniform and the war around us. He had trained me to wait, accept denial, look upon our precious hours together as found and fleeting. Nothing mattered except that he study for his medical school exams and teach physiology on the side to earn his living. Moody and dedicated, like my father, he was going to be a doctor, like my father. My love was almost ten years older than I. He already had his Doctor of Philosophy degree and soon would have his medical one— unusual feats for a poor boy from the ghettos of Brooklyn. He had fought his way alone for years and still lived with his old mother, whom he supported.

I adored every inch of his handsome, tweedy, pipe-smoking, curly, sandy-haired, blue-eyed, shaggy-browed presence; his careful, soft, life-was-real, life-was-earnest voice; and his speech sounding as if he had come from generations of New England country gentlemen. The hours he allowed for us to be together were stolen hours; I must never forget that, he taught me. Every good-bye was a loss to bear that made you stronger, every sunset a gift we should wonder if we deserved and might not enjoy again for some time—life was that serious for him. He taught me our hours together should feel as exalted, heart-paining, fleeting as a Chopin *étude* in a minor key. Sometimes he would do the unthinkable, throw caution to the winds, bring his books to the apartment, and stay with me the whole weekend! . . . While he memorized things like "islet of Langerhans" (masses of endocrine cells around the pancreas, that secrete insulin) . . . While I gleamed quietly and tiptoed about, secreting my dedication to our love by cooking, setting the table with the brass candlesticks, proving to him how good and patient I could be—I was *not* an unpredictable dreamer with a head full of crazy impulses, dance, love songs. . . . I was a serious student at the Juilliard School of Music. I would open my books, too, curl up in another corner of the room, and try to concentrate on orchestration, or the French that I was always flunking . . . strange, considering my musical ear. My stumbling about in the fields of that glorious language would always be related, somehow, to potholes belonging to me alone. My French teacher in high school was the only one who thought to sit with me when my mother died. French was the language of death, and later, of love to be punished for.

My second year at Juilliard was the year I

met my love from Brooklyn. Come the end
of May, I refused to go home to Massachusetts and vacation on the familiar beaches, as
Papa commanded. I insisted on remaining in
hot New York. So Papa said, All right, then
you have to find a job and support yourself
for the summer, and take a makeup course
in French, which you flunked again. I joined
the war effort and found a job in a factory
that made submarine parts. It took me no
time at all to master the drill press skill,
what with my piano finger dexterity. I
worked too fast for the assembly line and
was ordered to slow down by the foreman or
I would be ostracized, maybe even fired. Life
was difficult on the factory floor, dirty and
raucous, but good for the soul and country. I
reasoned. I didn't fit in at all, and the other
workers made no bones about it, particularly
the women. My measurements were 36-24-
36, my overalls too well made and new, and
the male operators found the full-length
back zipper of my form-fitting Lord & Tay-
lor *costume* irresistible. With the same
laughter as the men, the hefty, tough-talking
Gerties from the Bronx, there to earn a serious living and support families, watched me

flounder, blush, learn to protect myself. But it was all worth it, riding the subways at dawn to punch in the time clock by 6:00 A.M. Because on certain evenings I could see my love and walk the hot, soft-air streets with his arm about my waist, then make love in my little apartment, sometimes on wetted-down sheets, it was such a sweltering summer. Come August I had developed such an allergy to the oil that cooled the drill press that I was back home in Massachusetts, with my precious piano fingers so swollen and infected Papa had to spend hundreds of dollars to have me cured, by the best Harvard allergist, of course . . . and there went my French course, as well as my plan to sacrifice for love.

A year later, with my love: Isn't this wonderful! He's here! The two of us studying together . . . I couldn't concentrate for a second, it was so shatteringly delicious to make believe that we were married. And at a certain point, I would sense him putting his book down, feel his eyes on me, and we would make love. It was worth all the patience and waiting that he was trying to teach me. *I knew he loved me when we made love,* free, sweet, passionate, standing, sitting, in the shower—I was the key that unlocked his prison cell, I was the beauty, the chosen one. It was like a dozen Chopin pieces, some of them in major keys, when he exploded in me; afterward, with his blue eyes and mine, like children splashing in a pool. The orgasmic vibrations of lovers, the orgasm itself, if ever calibrated, would definitely be found to have the consonant sound of the intervals of major thirds and sixths, never minor; never the spare, formal fourths and fifths of Gregorian chant, or the intense dissonance of sevenths, no matter how diminished or augmented, even by Stravinsky.

Otherwise, time shared with my love was all down into the printed word, the hush of a public library; it was monks with curved spines bending over eggshell parchment, their ink squeezed from the petals of black tulips and deadly nightshade; or old rabbis squinting through the Dark Ages, poring over the latest-to-arrive-by-horseback interpretation of the Talmud, from some wise man far away. *That* was my love: Man must read and study, exercise his superior intelligence with words in black and white. All

else was unfocused and without consequence, stolen time.

Our love was two years old by 1943. He
had gone home with me for several weekends—he loved the fall in New England.
Papa almost approved. They got along very
well, for two men who were withdrawn and
careful about their words. Papa almost en-
tertained the thought that this was the man I
might marry someday if the planets were in
their right places.

My life was not like my neat little apartment. I was a sad, mystified girl, crying on
the telephone, pleading for visits with my
love: I'd be quiet as a mouse, he could study,
why did he have to take the long subway
ride to Brooklyn to his mother's house after
his classes? *"Your* work?" he would ask.
"Don't you have a piano exam coming up?"
"Oh, yes, that, my work . . . fine, fine."
"Be good, sugar," he'd say. "Maybe I can
find a few hours this weekend, next weekend.
. . ." Life is real, life is earnest, he would
remind me in different ways with a patient
but sometimes annoyed laugh, to get me off
my hook of tears. I was being unreasonable,
rebellious, wanting, lacking in self-reliance.

He didn't need that kind of weight, not with what *he* had to accomplish. Love was what you did when all other obligations were fulfilled.

I would put the telephone down, shaking from contact with his voice (better that than no voice), my chest heavy with longing and guilt. Not knowing it consciously, but unconsciously to the extreme: Was I not a proper girl from New England, with a Judaic-Christian signpost hammered into her at birth, through a tunnel that had been drilled from the top of her head to her anus —to keep her steady, to make sure she would always be a nontipping vessel for guilt to the brim? The chemical ingredients in happiness were *verboten,* the only things that could eat into her walls and cause them to break into hundreds of pathetic shards, with nothing left but the pole. How could one live being nothing but a pole for everyone to see? Particularly my love, who would be revolted by the sight and turn away, in case he might be, in some small way, to blame for destroying my cover. No, it was proper to be guilty, and ill to long for what could destroy you: happiness.

* * *

It was a week since I had seen my love. We were deep into the fall semester. I had never been an enthusiastic academic student. The shoes of formal learning had always been too tight; there was no last that fitted me properly. My head was either too fat (I was ahead of the class) or too thin (I wasn't there at all).

To hell with it; I was rushing to be where I wanted to be, where I was quite often—Café Society (the only college that made sense) . . . to study glorious jazz, the wonderful pianist Hazel Scott; the boogie-woogie masters Meade Lux Lewis, Pete Johnson; Art Tatum and Eddie Hayward; the folk singer Susan Reed with her long, red, silk hair and voice clear as a mountain stream; and many other "teachers" whose names escape me but who taught me the history of *song,* from the troubadours of the Aquitaine, composing their chansons and stories in the court of Eleanor's grandfather, to the songs Shakespeare heard and loved; to the Spanish, Russian, Irish, Scottish and German songs that had pointed the heart's way for centuries. I learned them the right way, close enough to touch.

Café Society and Max Gordon's Village Vanguard, which opened in 1939, were the only clubs in New York or anywhere else in the country where black and white could sit down together and enjoy American music. Café Society was the doing of Barney Josephson, the owner of the club. He couldn't get over the fact that the Cotton Club in Harlem (where Duke Ellington, Lena Horne, Cab Calloway, all of the black greats, performed) was a segregated club. The blacks had to sit in the back, even in Harlem. The jazz geniuses of the age could only be heard by a mostly white audience. Barney didn't approve of that, so he borrowed money, had famous American artists paint murals all over the walls, and created his own posh café in the Village, for all races, where jazz history was made the moment it opened.

How wonderful to live so close to your real "college."

My brother-in-law Bob was waiting for me with a table down front, as he had promised.

The air was electric, as it always was, filled with the expectation of being lifted out of your skeletal structure, organs flying free in all directions for a delectable while, particularly the heart. Skeletons and organs: everything my love was studying about in his mother's house deep in the Brooklyn ghetto he had fought his way out of, to fulfill his dream, to be a doctor. Nothing would keep him from that; he had come from too poor, too ordinary; he had worked too hard, studied too long, to allow any luring away, anything else to shake him hard. I missed his not sharing such evenings with me.

Bob and I liked being with each other—it was a nice family belonging, even if he wasn't my brother-in-law anymore.

Josh White, in the smoky, excited atmosphere, built his program to its highlight— "Strange Fruit," his handsome black face glistening under the hot stage lights. There wasn't a dry heart when the song was over. Everyone was stunned (again) by the shame of Man's cruelty and the power of a *song*. A *nigger* had been lynched in front of us, his only crime—that he was a *nigger;* and he

was swaying from the branch of a tree like a
strange fruit.

I wished my love were there so I could
grab his hand.

Before the evening started, Bob and I had
both noticed a young soldier sitting by himself at a table. Not a soldier, Bob corrected
me, a sailor, a British sailor. The lights went
down and Bob whispered to me: "Not a
sailor, an officer in the British Navy." "What
a shame for him to be sitting alone in a foreign country," I said. "Should you invite
him to join us?"

The music started and we forgot the
young man alone. At the end of "Strange
Fruit," a figure came toward us.

"Would you mind If I joined you two?
This kind of music is no fun alone—he's
magnificent, isn't he?"

Bob said, "By all means . . ."

I looked up at the stranger. "Funny, we
were thinking the same thing. We noticed
you sitting alone."

"I know you did," he said. "And then the
lights went down." He pulled up a chair
without any awkwardness; it seemed the
most logical thing for him to join us. Bob

introduced himself and me, "This is my sister-in-law . . ." A little smile broke on the
young man's face. And what a face it was.
Bob and I looked at each other, saying si-
lently, Is that handsome, or isn't it, my
God!? He was in his dress uniform, dark
blue, English-cut, slightly rumpled (the English didn't have the cloth quality of the
American uniform), dull brass-buttoned, an
officer's stripe on his sleeves, a long white
silk aviator's scarf hanging loosely down his
front, and he laid his cap, with the encrusted
gold and red insignia of the King pinned
above its visor, on the table. His hair was the
color of corn silk and his blue eyes were
clear but filled with a fatigue, a distance I
had never seen before—a look that separates
a battle-weary soldier from others.

"Welcome, stranger from a far-off land," I
said, and we all laughed.

"How did you find Café Society?" Bob
asked.

"Saw it in your papers. I'm mad about
American jazz, I have quite a bit of it in
London, on record, and Josh White's, too.
We're on leave just for one night, and I
wasn't going to miss hearing him in person if

I could help it. Funny," he said, "three of my mates and I were standing on the corner out there, near that little park? We were coming here together and they decided they'd rather go somewhere just to drink and whoop it up. You know, cut up a bit, men on leave." He grinned. "We stood there discussing it. I almost went with them, but my left foot said, 'No. When will you ever be back in New York City again?' It stepped off the curb, heading south, and I waved good-bye, see you later, blokes."

"Do you mind being asked where you're from, what you've been doing, and where you're going?" Bob asked gently.

"Hometown, London, sir," the young man said with a laugh. "Only child, haven't been home forever. In the Air Arm of the British Navy, sir, Lieutenant Kenneth Hanson, at your service. Why am I in your wonderful town? Our aircraft carrier broke down in the North Atlantic. We're all fixed and ready to leave tomorrow. The carrier is sitting out there in your Hudson River. . . . Where we're going, I can't tell you; most of the time we don't know ourselves, until we're there. Where we were? Africa, European Theater, even the Pacific . . ." His eyes stopped being cocky and got that sad fatigue back. "For two years," he added.

"It's pretty tough out there, isn't it," Bob said.

"Yes . . ."

"Are you a ship's officer, Kenneth?"

"Bob, you're being nosy," I joked.

"No, no, it's all right," the young man responded. "I'll ask you questions, too, just wait. Everything American interests me, I warn you. . . .

"I'm a single-fighter airplane pilot, is what I am," he said casually and flung his long white silk scarf around his neck. "See? It has its compensations . . . glamor. When could I ever wear a white silk scarf except to the opera?"

The band was playing dance music between Josh White's song sets. Lieutenant Kenneth Hanson suddenly stood up, bowed slightly to me, and with the slightest twinkle, said to Bob, "May I have your permission to dance with your sister-in-law?"

A tall, ingenuous, lonely, incredibly handsome young man led me out to the small dance floor, put his arms about me sweetly, and off we went. One dance, two dances. With the third, he leaned down to rest his cheek on mine; our bodies fitted, fitted together as if we had known each other for a long time. I loved to dance. It was the perfect dance. In war, everything larger than life. I suspended guilt.

My love, studying somewhere in Brooklyn, wasn't dancing inclined. It made him uncomfortable, and he had never had the time—dance was play. (I had been brought up to feel that dance, any kind of dance, was tinged with the magic of the gods. The body in movement—the oldest art form in the world, except for the beating of drums and the sound of a reed.) At some point my eyes sought out Bob, sitting at our table, and his eyebrows were raised, in disapproval or amusement or vague envy, I wasn't sure which, maybe all of it. It was an important look in retrospect, Bob being Bob, sensitive to me always—he saw me happy, having fun. But he wasn't. When the dance music ended and Josh White continued his songs, Bob was superfluous; he and I knew it. Something strange was transpiring, in the most precipitous way, as only magic can.

Bob decided to leave. "Have a good time, children," he said wryly. "Get her home safely," he said to the aviator. My heartbeat quickened. I looked at Bob: Should you? Should I? I have no idea who he is, I've never done this before, and I certainly shouldn't be doing it now. But Bob gave me no indication of noticing my small panic.

"I'll take good care of Smoky, don't worry, Robert, brother-in-law." Kenneth stood up and clicked his heels, aping formality. "And thank you for bringing her. . . ."

"Smoky?" I said.

"Yes, I've decided you're Smoky. May I call you that?"

"Meet you in London, someday . . . in front of the British Museum? God willing," Bob said, giving the uniformed elbow a quick grasp. He kissed me on the forehead and left.

Circling, circling, inner arabesques, court dances of held-in grace, waltzes in the heart . . . outer air fluttering with slide, glide, tenderness; he seemed transported in stolen time, and I was some treasure found. It was unbelievable: "Someday my prince will come. . . ." We danced some more, left the café, walked up the street, and I pointed to where I lived, "the windows with the grill-work there; there's a grand piano in the window and it gets peed on." We laughed. I was not going to ask him in; he didn't want to be asked in, he wanted to swim, sink, drown in New York. He hailed a cab and we drove up to Central Park, talking, talking, New York ablaze with light, no light, a strange city of dream I had never been in before. He hailed a hansom cab in front of the Plaza Hotel and we rode around the park for hours, talking, talking, a hand was taken, a cheek stroked. . . . "Around the park again," he ordered, "until the horse can't take it anymore."

He had been in the war for almost two years, he said; fighter pilots were given eighteen months; everything from then on was borrowed. "I'm going to try to make it," he said simply. "I know it now. . . ."

Something cynical in me, spoiled and rotten, disbelieving the directness, something so used to veiled feelings, sophisticated protective feints and guardedness, made me pull back inside with a "My God, what a come-on, a new way to get someone into bed—make love before we die!" Or was I close to war for the first time, and it made life too beautiful and horrifying, the thought of this blond Billy Budd to be crucified, with his clear brow, fatigued eyes alive with loving anything that could deny the dark.

Around, around the park. "May I kiss you, Smoky? I won't if you don't want me to, but I shall never forget this night, and you, and Josh White, and your history, the *nigger* hanging from the tree; all people share a lot, the way they can be cruel to each other." He suddenly laughed. "Poor Robert, we ruined his evening, didn't we? Give him my apologies when you see him. . . ."

He kissed me and I let him. We kissed as if he were going off to war, which he was! I kissed him as if I were all mothers, sisters, wives, sweethearts in the world. Reality hit me like an ugly accident. We kissed, for trips and trips around the park, until it had to be over. It was dawn. He didn't want to know anything about me except my music, where I was born, my parents, my sister, my friends . . . nothing about whether I had a love. But he told me: "There's a girl in London, but now I'm not sure, I don't want to be sure. *We've* met, haven't we! It was that left foot of mine stepping into the gutter and walking toward Café Society. We can't say that wasn't a miracle, not after tonight, Smoky. . . ."

He brought me home, we kissed good-bye. "We won't say the word," he said. "It's bad luck. Let's just say, 'I love you'. . . . That's true, isn't it?" He laughed with such delight, it was kind of mad, and he walked away from the door of my apartment, jamming his British cap onto his blond, shining head of hair, off to join his squadron on the aircraft carrier, and where they were headed for, only Hitler's Luftwaffe might know.

I curled up on the couch in my little apartment, with my cat and my brass candlesticks, my piano and my books, all as unfamiliar as if I had just arrived from London to a quaint student's digs in the United States of America.

Breathless with deceit and guilt, sprung from my moorings, I put my head between my legs and wept for someone I would never see again, with whom I had fallen in love, as in fairy tales and romance novels. Worse, I couldn't even imagine him anywhere! I knew nothing of ghost ships moving through icy fog, bombers above them, submarines below them flitting like man-made sharks. I knew nothing about dogfights in the glorious blue sky. A clear sky!—a lift to the heart, another day! But for the single-fighter plane it only meant clear visibility to kill or be killed. I couldn't believe I had been kissed by such a one. I knew nothing of his reality; therefore he wasn't real, I had dreamed it. . . .

Better to make believe I had dreamed such a slightly mad embracing of two souls, entangled in the air as if they were the tails of riotously colored kites, before a wind blew them on their way.

Two Selves in Love

Two months later, settled back into engineering my overloaded train up the familiar but always treacherous mountain passes, used to the cargo shifting on the twists and turns of waiting for my love to call from his mother's house in Brooklyn, practicing a Bach Suite and a difficult Schumann piece for a piano exam, trying to understand the variables of acoustics, the architecture of orchestration . . . the phone rang.

An unrecognizable voice began to sing: " 'Put your arms around me, honey, hold me tight. . . .' " Then an English accent: "Smoky! I'm here! The ship broke down again. I knew it! I knew that we'd meet again! We have the weekend, I've got my parachute with me, have to keep it somewhere safe. The carrier's being towed to Virginia and we left our planes in Pennsylvania. May I? May I see you, my darling Smoky? I couldn't write, we weren't anywhere I could mail a love letter. I will deliver it in person."

Silence. I couldn't say a word.

"Smoky? Don't you remember? Have I rung up a wrong number?" His voice had faded in confusion.

"You're here?" It had to sink in. "You're alive and here? . . ." I almost whispered, in case someone in the room who wasn't, might hear. The "alive" came out like a practical merciless accountant making a cruel assessment of what should or should not be added or subtracted, what penalties would have to be extracted if my voice screamed in joy: "How wonderful!"

I made an instantaneous decision to lie. Not to the voice on the phone but to everything else! I jumped off the train of maybe a quiet dinner with the brass candlesticks, maybe a call from Brooklyn or outside a hospital ward, from my love, the doctor;

maybe I'd pass or fail Bach and Schumann, the mathematics of the vibrations of sound in the lower registers. My voice shrilled out high and clear, "How wonderful!"

An hour later, a blond stranger flung his parachute to the floor and hugged me as if Wagner were rewriting Tristan's entrance just for him—a modern Viking in khakis; quicker, brighter, with subtle rhythms; sliding, gliding laughs, the inner arabesque, the outer air waltzing, the grace of court dances. . . . I hadn't imagined it that night of our meeting in Café Society. There wasn't one evil cackle of prophecy, not one portent of shadow or doom or waiting or longing in the little room. The room was shocked by its instantaneous repainting: in the color of joy the way it should be—the absence of any other tint but its own.

I looked at the parachute, a bulky bundle of tan, silky nylon, a laundry bag that was the difference between life and death. My little cat went up to it to investigate the smells of God knows what—the North Sea, Africa, London Bridge?

"No! No claws, please, I beg of you!" He swooped up the cat in his arms. "Hail Mary, full of grace, not Smoky's cat, oh, no, not now, maybe someday when I give you the order, dearie: 'Tear it apart!'" He asked where the parachute could be put out of the way, where it wouldn't be tripped on or harmed.

"My most prized possession this year," he said, suddenly sober. "We have to lug them with us. Everything's in different places, the damn carrier, American-made, it's always breaking down; our planes somewhere else . . . 'a friggin' mess,' one of your port officers said when we limped in."

"Where were you coming from?"

"Cold and far away. I can't say, Smoky, sorry. . . . I'm not going to think about it for two whole days!"

He had a present for me. "I wanted to pick mimosa for you in a place I know in southern France, but I couldn't get there, somehow. I went to a couple of flower shops here, but they didn't have mimosa," he said with a grin. "So this will have to do." He pawed out some rumpled sheet music from his knapsack. "We heard it on our short-wave, straight from the United States: 'Put

your arms around me, honey, hold me tight.
. . .' I love it, boppy, silly, crazy. . . ."

He pulled me down on the couch and held
me tight for two days.

I learned that he had been in college when
the ax fell. "A lad, a mere wanton lad,
snatched from his mother's teat." His father
was a bus driver; his mother, a lady who had
fallen in love "beneath her" and married despite the family shouting. "A good man, a
dear man, and obviously a very handsome
man, like me," he teased. I couldn't tell
whether he was pulling my leg . . . it
didn't matter. He hadn't read as much as he
should have, he said, but that would all
come later, if there would be a later. "Of
course there will be a later; I love you,
Smoky. . . ."

He believed he was "a wishy-washy socialist," he wasn't near being an intellectual, he
apologized. "What *you* are used to, all the
music and books and new art. I'm just a
dumb Limey."

I denied any relation to *intellectual* and
laughed. "Wait till you meet my sister. I'm
the lazy one in my family."

"London is somewhere else, a little busy

at the moment," he pardoned England and himself bitterly.

The royal family, how could socialists love a royal family? I asked the usual American question.

Ah, Americans just don't understand. The *family* is so silly, comfortable, they're our old shoes, our history, old-fashioned, dumpy, stuffy, and we love the pomp. Don't you? The purple and gold, the silks and satins, prancing horses, royal carriages, everyone's a child when they roll by. . . . "Don't take my fairy tale away from me, it's mine," he mock-pleaded. "They're worth every pound we pay them, for the fantasy." He looked at me, surprised I wouldn't understand. "They go on forever, the perfect, middle-class family, a thousand years of tradition and continuity . . . of love, murder, greed, valor, sacrifice, bravery, common law, the Magna Charta, freedom, conquest, victory. . . . Won't you let me convince you I'm wonderful?

"I'm an Englishman, Smoky, you can't deny me my royal family, it's my teddy, my toy, I sleep with it, I wake with it, I might even die for it. . . . But I won't, because I'm going to marry an American girl and bring her back to England!"

We left the apartment for a trip in an outside world that seemed as strange and new-feeling as the night we met and went around Central Park in a carriage.

We went to The Cloisters in Fort Tryon Park, at the tip of Manhattan. It was a museum of medieval art housed in a recreation of a Romanesque chapel and monastic cloisters overlooking the Hudson River. I think I suggested it because it was the closest thing to his Europe, the hush of the old and beautiful, and it was perched on the top of our city, like a wise old bird.

We wandered hand in hand, like two waifs, or a benighted prince and princess doomed by circumstance, through the stone and shadow of The Cloisters. He described every moment of it in a letter written weeks later—how we had come out of a chapel, to a courtyard with a floor of daffodils, and he needed to wander off alone because he felt like crying, but suddenly he panicked, he had lost me; and a gull overhead was crying and he had thought it was himself crying. . . . He ran looking for me, thinking he had dreamed me, but there I was: "a tall, cool girl with long, dark hair, standing outside on the parapet, looking down at the Hudson River meandering like Gypsies. You stretched out your hand to me and the nightmare stopped," he wrote.

I remembered that moment very well—of a battle-weary, scared young man filled with love and loss. I remembered thinking: That's what we do to them in war, scrape their souls to the bone, suck out the marrow, and turn away. And the way he looked at me, breathless, white-faced, saying, "I thought I'd lost you . . ." Suddenly a smile, a handsome face filled with courage and calm, and he kissed me with such a surety and sweetness.

I *had* to tell him about my love, the student-doctor.

The disclosure didn't faze him at all. "I have a rival? Well, I'd like to meet him; I probably shall one day. He must be fine if you *thought* you loved him. It'll be a fair fight, but I'm the one who's going to win."

That evening he left to go to God knows where—security forbade him telling me—

and who knew whether I would ever see him again.

It was a glassy time reflected in tricky mirrors for both of us. He had spiritually crash-landed into my life, and I had to pick up the pieces. He might physically crash *out there* and not land anywhere—there would not even be pieces. He left me, terrified for both of us. The pain of my guilt was excruciating. After he left, I sat at my piano under the window and cried and played until the keys were too slippery to respond.

It was a different good-bye this time. Some kind of crazy house of love had had its foundation dug. I had another house to tear down, if I had the courage to be alone and wait. Wait. Wait. It seemed that I would always have to wait for love. I had to choose what kind of loving I wanted to wait for.

Choices

THE pupils in Willow's eyes had taken possession of their entire orbs and turned them into blazing black opals.

"Does He know about all of this?"

"Of course Jules does; it happened a long time ago. But, if you must know, there was a time when Jules felt very threatened by his memory, my special love for him."

"Did he die?"

"It felt worse than death at the time. Memory of him didn't die."

Willow didn't like something about this at all. I don't think she liked memory; it usurped her Present, for that was all she had, being Cat. She jumped off the top of the buffet where she had sat motionless thus far, watching me chart my course through the fog, and jumped into my lap to be stroked. It was very perceptive of her to feel that I needed her as much as she needed me, at that moment. "If things had not happened the way they evidently did," she purred, "I might not have been here at all, or you, or anything I know this Time around. I only have so much to understand with, about Time. I can feel an aeon of earth Time, but human years are a mystery, and I might add, more dangerous. I don't like death talk; I don't want to hear any more—"

"It's not death talk, Willow, it's life talk, and you *are* going to hear what happened, because you started it, with your pushing me about the fork, what's with the fork. You know how curious you say you are about human ways of loving, just in case, I don't know what, but just in case you might have a try at it one day, my pet, and see how well you do, given the chance. I am trying to show you that the fog can be parted, again, again, and each time with more truth. *Your* favorite word, isn't it?"

She was trying to maintain her back to me, her I'm-making-believe-I'm-not-listening-position, but her curiosity was too strong and she turned abruptly to look at me: "All right, what *about* the fork that made you go back into the fog, in the first place!?"

❧   ❧

Letters began to arrive from the censored nowhere of war. "Darling Smoky, your student, how I envy him in the same city, near to you." . . . "I wonder if you'll throw me over and marry the student." . . . "I'm writing to you from the cold, everything cold. I think of your body, soft, beautiful as I have ever touched. Tell me we have a forever; it's your decision. No, it isn't! My family motto is *à fin.* It must be for you and me . . ."

His letters bore H.M.S. *Censor*'s seal, that's all. Where was he? I sent my letters to His Majesty's Admiralty in London.

It was the late fall of 1943. Sicily and the southern Italian mainland had surrendered in September. Had he been there? The Germans had surrendered in Stalingrad, I knew he wasn't there. The war was changing color

—the German submarine fleet was now almost destroyed. Is that where he had been and was? In the North Atlantic? Was that why the aircraft carrier could limp back to an American port? Was that the "cold, everything cold"? Or was it the North Seas, Wales, Ireland for safety?

I felt as if I were writing to my imagination.

I was in love with two men because I had two selves. One needed to feel unworthy, rejected, and deserved being held at arm's length. For was I not too mercurial, impractical, running after maturity as if it were Alice's White Rabbit? The other self wanted to be loved—soaring, classic, pure, lyric, like a Mozart melody, the only Truth, and I deserved its Light, its shield against Shadow! A love only between the covers of a book, and I had found it. It was mine!

No, I must close the door on soaring free, I didn't have the guts to love a stranger who was going to be shot down and die. I would rather love someone who shot me down daily but was near and familiar. I was a Jewish, New England, snob-coward. My aviator was an unknown, unschooled, a Christian, someone who used the word *forever*. A Jew doesn't know *forever*. My feelings shocked me even more than my schizophrenia, they were so provincial, fundamentalist-narrow. I had ghettoized my feelings, out of fear, and they numbed me.

His letters stopped coming. The silence from the Saxon gave me the courage to make a choice. He was dead, we had no connection but for the remembrance of fantasy hours. I tried to make them fade, even as the self that belonged to him mourned secretly. I sat in a corner of my room, watching my "student," the familiar, memorize his way through the illnesses of the body, and I made peace with what I deserved—to be obedient, grateful for the known, love on hold, but love, that was clear. There was his gaze, occasionally, to rest his eyes: Ah, you're good, sugar, you're learning what life is about.

"Darling! We're in Maine! We're flying down the coast today! See you tomorrow! God, I can't wait. Did you get my letters, too hot to handle? Did you have a merry Christmas? Happy New Year, love, a few months late."

I waited for his arrival the next day, like a condemned one.

That afternoon the mail brought his letters lost and found. His love rose off the pages, filling the apartment with the seditious and forbidden. I was a liar, a cheat, a spy. My hands trembled from the speaking rising off the pages, the writer straining to touch me: "I'm reading *Main Street;* please send me all of Mark Twain, American poets, if it's not too much trouble. I must learn as much about you as I can. . . . I'm also devouring American history, cowboys, Indians. . . ."

Christopher Street was again filled with a fallout of crazy stars. Plop! The parachute in the corner, the smell of the sky and sea, the khaki of live heroes and dead men.

"Do you know what happened on the way down from Maine, Smoky? We were flying in formation when I realized we would be over Peabody. I asked permission to break formation and fly low so that I could see where you were born . . . and Burt, our squadron leader, said yes. The whole squadron knows how mad I am about you, that's all I talk about. So that's what I did, and if anyone wanted to give a certain British naval Air Arm squadron emergency orders, it would have been impossible. The war was on hold for a few minutes over Peabody, Massachusetts. Everyone was singing into their intercoms, at the top of their lungs, teasing me with your folk song 'On top of Old Smoky, all cozy and warm' . . . while I flew over Peabody, looking for your father's house."

"How could you possibly know where?"

"Silly girl, of course I didn't know where to look, but my heart felt close to where you were born—one of the white houses down there. . . . I grazed the treetops, with your name on the nose of the plane. Did I write you that I had named my plane? I flew over the beginning of Smoky, is what I did."

"The whole squadron singing 'all cozy and warm' instead of 'all covered with snow'? How embarrassing! You're all mad."

"Can you blame us? I *am* mad. It's making me ill—missing you, wanting to touch you, loving you."

He had a surprise for me, he said. He was going to take me to dinner in England the next day, we'd be on *his* land, in *his* house, where he felt comfortable. They had flown

their planes to New Jersey and the carrier
was in the Hudson, he explained patiently.
There would be no time for love this day,
since he had to report to the ship, but tomorrow there would be a tender waiting for me
at the Pier on Forty-second Street. It would
bring me to the carrier and I would be in
England. He had arranged everything with
his leader. The squadron was to have the
night off, there would be no one on board
but the cook, his helpers, and a skeleton
crew. The cook was going to make the finest
dinner for . . . he hugged me, "For Naval
Lieutenant Hanson and his girl, the American music student with the green eyes."

To the middle of the Hudson I was taken,
somewhere upriver. A remote ghostly picture behind me. Manhattan was the imagined now, where there was an apartment on
Christopher Street, and far off, around the
bend of the island, past the Statue of Liberty,
was Brooklyn and a man with deep, faraway
eyes, smoking his pipe, studying in his mother's house. He might call, but I wasn't *there*.
    Waiting for me on deck in his dress uni-
form, blond hair gleaming in the dark, very

formal and serious he was, with his calling down, "Welcome to the British Isles." A few Limey sailors registered curious but polite looks: Officer's girl coming on board.

Everything had a quiet smile as I climbed up the ladder.

The officers' dining room of the carrier could have been Oxford or the Harvard Club —a hushed mood of dark-wood paneling, brass, drapes; civilized, gentrified; a deserved dining room for gentlemen warriors picked from the sons of bus drivers miners, or dukes. It was England's pride.

One table in the empty dining room was set for a special fuss dinner—shining glasses, silver, flowers in a bowl. A steward hovered over us with quiet discretion; he came and went, pouring wine and bringing a wonderfully cooked meal of Dover sole.

"They treat us well when we're not in the air or barracks somewhere cold," Ken said with a smile. His whole demeanor was different; something solid, validated, had replaced a worn-out Launcelot on the run. He was on home ground and real to himself, if not to me.

The cook came out to pay his respects and

be thanked for all the trouble he had gone to, for "the American girl." Everyone on the carrier had known what the dinner was for, what I did not know as I lifted a fork to my lips. . . .

"Will you do me the honor of marrying me, Smoky, the next time we come back, if I can get the necessary papers together and receive permission?"

The perfect war. There had to be a perfect love until it was won. He had convinced himself to love, so as not to die. That's what I was for: to keep him from dying. Cynicism had poisoned me for only one reason. To protect my fear. No, two reasons, and I would have to tell him. I was pregnant, and it wasn't his fault. I was going into my second month, and we hadn't seen each other for three. I was a cheat, a liar, unworthy. I was not my father's daughter, I was no one.

How can your heart break and keep on beating while your head is slowly saying no?

"Why not? Is it the student? He's won? I can't believe that, I know you love me, I know by your letters, your eyes. . . . It's the only thing I do know!"

Tears streamed down my cheeks. I put the fork down.

"It doesn't matter. Have the baby! I will love it as if it were our first because it's out of you, the medical student be damned. If you don't want it . . . no one can tell you what to do with your body. Smoky, listen . . ."

"I can't listen."

"Listen! I know I have two strikes against me. You don't know who I am, you know who *he* is. But I'm going to make you *see* who I am. I might . . . I might die, yes, but I'd like to know you're my wife while I try my damndest not to. Providence will bring me back, you wait and see."

He took my hands in his. "If it does happen . . . just think, girl, if I get shot down, you'll have my pension, you could finish your studies with it, make yourself the best, compose the most beautiful music, and I'll be with you for a while. . . . I thought it all out in a barracks in Ireland. And if I don't die? After the war you'll come to England and we'll live happily ever after."

"You're crazy."

"Yes. About you, forever."

"Do not use that word! That's not fair!"

"I know it isn't."

He was smiling. He saw through me to my bone and still loved me. "I called your father in New England. I asked for your hand in marriage."

"You what? He doesn't even know you exist! What did he say?"

(I could hear Papa's call to me: Who was that young man with the accent, who called me? What are you doing? What about your classes? [You bad girl!] What have you done now?)

"What did he say? Was he polite?"

"Very. We chatted, I told him who I was, about my family, the war, he's right up on it. He said, 'Thank you for calling, young man. I'll talk to her.'

"We love each other, don't we?" he said matter-of-factly. "The truth, Smoky, time won't countenance anything else."

"I love you, I said. "But I'm full of shadows. . . ."

"I know," he said. "I'm going to blow them away one by one when the war is over."

How I wished . . . I didn't deserve to wish.

"Another cliché, love: All's fair in love and war. I'll damn wait until you get your head straight. I love that head. I will wait."

We both took the tender back. I never felt as unworthy, dirty, heavy, caught by my own nature and nature itself. I was pregnant! How dare I dare to love! I believed in nothing but my masochism, my dependency on grudging love. I loved him as I had never loved anyone, yet that lovely freedom was beyond my reach, it was not for me. There were sins I had to pay for. They were there when I was born; my mother's eyes had told me that. My father was still telling me. A young man was telling me otherwise, but I didn't believe him. The only reality I felt at home with was my *badness.*

He had left his parachute in my apartment the day before, knowing the squadron had to pick up their planes in New Jersey and meet the carrier in the Atlantic. He had planned the marriage proposal, the happy trip back, the last hour of stolen time. It was not as he had planned. I had a premonition that it would be the last time we would ever see each other.

I had another premonition, a correct one. That my love, the student, as my other love respectfully called him, had been in the apartment.

There were pipe ashes in an ashtray! Of course he had a key, for two years! God, let him not return. No, he wouldn't, it was almost midnight, he was too organized for that. Possible skulduggery aside, one had to sleep, there was a long subway ride home, classes the next day.

How unusual for him just to drop in. He must have come all the way from Brooklyn, perhaps he had sensed something. There had been no tentative, sad call from me for two days: "How are you, where are you?" Where was his tame moth?

And there was the parachute sitting in the middle of the room. A laundry bag? My mind was wild with weaving lies: It was a friend of Bob's, a flier, who'd left it . . . we all went out to dinner. (I would have to call Bob and ask him to lie for me. I'd have to.)

Just go still . . . and cry. After the good-bye to someone who wouldn't be in safe classrooms, but on the high seas, in the high clouds, chasing shadows bigger than mine.

The next evening, I was in bed and the door opened. My love the student walked into the dark. He stood over me.

What was I doing with a parachute in my apartment? Whose was it? It was not a laundry bag! *Whose was it!?*

A beautiful young man's! I was furious at being treated like a child! I didn't lie well. I wept and turned my face to the wall, waiting for my captor to clang the door and leave my prison cell.

But he didn't. He stood there. Then he came close to the bed. I had betrayed him. He knew everything without being told. Not everything. (He didn't know I was pregnant by him.) The precious, stolen hours he had invested in me had been sullied. I was a whore, he whispered. The controlled one, the one who knew life is real, life is earnest . . . *blew his top*. He hit me three times about the head, growled "Bitch!" and left.

I was dizzy with shock and pain. My curly, sandy-haired love with the deep-blue inside eyes, my pipe-smoking, tweedy lover of sunsets and falling leaves, my love the healer, had hurt me!

Mozart was dead. Vulgarity had been let loose and could never be poured back into the bottle. I got dressed, ran out into the street, and banged on the door of a friend who lived nearby. He knew of my Englishman, and he had spent many evenings with me and my student. He knew everything and tried to give me solace. I had lost my way, he said; I had to get back to music, work, study, the only real satisfactions. "Do yourself a favor. Fuck love for a while, you don't know who you are yet, so how can anyone else? You're too talented for this shit."

How to dignify a love, even if it had been torn to pieces? My two years of longing for something real with my student from Brooklyn was now an aborted fetus. He came back and studied again in the armchair and I set the table again with the brass candlesticks. He forgave me; I was not a whore, I was my father's prodigal daughter, and his. He didn't help me pay for the abortion because it wasn't his (he thought). He didn't say it in so many words. He said, "That's your problem, not *mine.* Anyway, I don't have the money, on my student-loan salary. You ought to know that." The subject was never discussed again. I borrowed the money from a modern dancer whose classes I played for, as well as composing for her concert pieces. Papa had me on a very short string, I always had to work for pin money. How else does one learn about the work ethic and responsibility? It took me a year of playing for dance classes to pay back the loan for the abortion.

Oppressed women don't leave easily, especially when they love their oppressors. And how my self that loved the student wanted to be near him, be worthy of him. And how the other self secretly dreamed of someone else . . . somewhere on a sea . . . in an airplane a second away from death. There were no letters for months, but I wrote anyway, as if the act of writing would ensure his being alive.

It was never the same again with the student. I was just as lonely and needing, yet *changed* despite my cowardly choice of wanting his silence and forgiveness and everything as it was, before the romantic myth-warrior with his long silk scarf woke me

from my long sleep with his kiss and promise
of "forever."

Be happy when you can.

The aircraft carrier returned. He had not
died. His letters must have gotten lost. My
letters were magic, they had kept him alive. I
lived my duality with no guilt this time.

Tears came to his eyes when I told him of
the abortion. There was change between us,
too, maybe a return to sanity because of
what *he* knew lay ahead. It was 1944. We
were now old friends who loved each other.
The war was pushing toward massive Allied
plans—it was in the air, and he knew more
than he could tell me. Be happy when you
can was his game plan, too. He was actually
on leave for a whole week.

I took my Englishman to Washington, to
meet Elizabeth. She was teaching modern
dance there and living alone after her divorce from Bob. How amused she was to
learn that Bob had been there at the beginning, when we had met at Café Society. We
told her all about it, the star-crossed love
that was now a year old.

It was a beautiful week. We were with

family. Even if I had not shared my pain with Elizabeth, she worried for me. I was the little sister, off the track as usual, but she could see, happy this time. She liked Ken. He was amazed to see how much we resembled each other, Elizabeth the light one, me the dark. Now he had two of them, *but I was his love.* We were normal young people for the first time, romping through Rock Creek Park with Lady, Elizabeth's English setter; sitting at Abraham Lincoln's feet, kissing in the shadows of the stone pillars heavy with my American history.

He proposed to me once more. I told him I could not marry him. "I don't have the guts." This time he accepted it.

I never saw him again after that glorious week. And yet there was one more time that his carrier limped back for repairs. He had called the friend I had run to after being beaten. Ken wanted to see someone I knew, but not me; it was too painful for him. So he went to Washington and slept with Elizabeth! I learned that years later, from Elizabeth. He needed one of the sisters, and she had allowed it. By then, he was crazed with war and felt his time was up. He had survived for over two years, and the odds were against him.

It was the end of May 1944 when he left for the last time and wrote my friend from the carrier heading for Europe. He wrote that when he realized Smoky meant no and had chosen the medical student (I had not), he knew he was leaving for *something catastrophic*. He broke down on the way back, broke out in boils, from nervous exhaustion, panic, and loss.

He was shot down off the coast of France.

But he didn't die. He was captured and spent the last year of the war in a German prisoner-of-war camp. He wrote all of that to my friend, not to me. I belonged to someone else.

But he was safe!

I didn't belong to someone else. I hadn't chosen. When I was young . . .

I moved away from Christopher Street and its memories of parachutes and golden love, brass candlesticks and medical books, suffocating duality . . . and with the urging of friends, settled into the top floor of a brownstone on Sixteenth Street, with skylights, sun, air.

Across the floor were my friends who were part of the heady tumult of the mid-1940s—artists, dancers, painters, musicians. Spanish Civil War songs, opera, the latest modern music filled the grand stairwell of the brownstone. Wine was the only drink anyone could afford. Vodka was for grand occasions, and parties always ended with wonderful dancing, dizzying tangos, improvised plays. Bill and Elaine de Kooning were there, never with any money, always borrowing and for good reason. Bill had decided he would not sell a painting for under five thousand dollars, even if it took years for that to happen. He was obviously correctly arrogant in trusting his genius. I managed to graduate from Juilliard, and then paid five dollars an hour to study composition with Lennie Bernstein, who had just arrived in New York from Harvard and was in analysis, he said, because he didn't know what he wanted to be, a composer, a pianist, or a conductor! (among other worries, I'm sure). I played for Martha Graham's dance classes and composed for Jean Erdmann, who was married to Joseph Campbell, a professor at Sarah Lawrence, whose passion for and teachings of mythology would soon enrich a generation of artists and finally the world. John Cage, composer, joker, mushroom collector, mystic, original of the minimalists, was writing his music for prepared piano. I played one of his compositions in a modern dance concert and had to prepare the piano before the lights went down—changing the vibrations of the strings by inserting pennies, felt, paper, all measured with a ruler; it was nerve-racking. (That was before John had decided that silence could be the real music, or the randomness of switching twelve radios off and on, the art of man-made sound.)

"Roosevelt is dead!" The country wept in the streets. V-Day came. The country wept again, this time with joy. But we weren't finished with the perfect war yet. Hiroshima was around the corner—the beginning of my maturity and the world's.

From the wasting of people and land to get over to Jordan, the dream of Moses realized; from the Greek and Roman and Egyptian conquests for freedom *or* greed, fertile land and power; from Mongol horses flying across Asia or Celts coming down, going back, crossing oceans; from the Crusades' raping of land and people in the name of Christ; from dukes and popes and kings and queens ravaging in the name of righteousness and fiefdoms; from peasants revolting and peasants squashed, revolutions born and revolutions buried; from Germany's twisted national psyche needing to be *Germany Above All,* even if it meant the death of millions; from little Japan, always with a frightened eye toward China, turning the fright into insatiable conquering (Japan: a freak of nature, with the DNA of *samurai* bred into its bone, whether dive-bombing into ships in Pearl Harbor or into the dazzling technological age that was to come) . . .

It was all when the world was young, before the atomic bomb and Hiroshima. And when my love from Brooklyn was slowly fading away.

He had betrayed me, too. But only in a way. Hadn't I deserved it? he reasoned. He had been dating a fellow medical student for a year and somehow managed to keep it from me. Well, that was easy . . . he had trained me to accept lonely time for years.

He had stayed, at the end, he said, only because he was worried about my constitution, how I would take the news. He was marrying a lovely woman, steady as a rock. I would like her, he said.

This little grain of changing, moving sand was free. *My* war was over. I had also lost a son. The reputable doctor (I was lucky to find him) who had performed the illegal abortion had told me that the fetus was a boy.

Where to put love? Into music, for quite a while. I could hear Papa breathing a sigh of relief in Massachusetts.

❧ ❧

"So much for holding a silver fork in my hand, Willow."

"So much for human memory," she said. "I promise I won't be so snappy about it anymore, comparing it with my brilliant ability to perceive a situation in a second."

"You got it all, didn't you."

"You know, he sounded like he was the kind of He who would have had my pan clean and my breakfast ready in the morning."

"Which he?"

"The English one!"

"You're probably right."

"I know I'm right, but I also know I'll never tease you again about being human."

She pricked her ears up. Someone was going to ring the bell. She always knew it before it happened. I'd have to hang out the window to see what she saw before it happened: someone at the downstairs door. When we were away, she knew when we were coming back at two hundred miles. We were told that by her cat-sitter. "She always gets *antsy* about two and a half hours before you arrive," the cat-sitter once told us. "Then I figured it out: That's just how long it took you to drive down from the Berkshires! And there you were, at the door, just as she said you'd be."

Jules rang from downstairs. She looked at me and fanned her ears impatiently. "There, you see?"

She also knew guests would arrive in a half hour, because she retired to a bedroom where she could listen to the voices and decide whether she liked them or not, whether she would come out or not, do a somersault or not. Since it was a real fuss dinner with the old silver, not Japanese stainless steel, I was sure she would join us. Willow was a party girl; she liked to dress up and wear jewelry. Kelly would be around Jules's neck whether it was silver or steel.

She had something to tell me before she left my lap: "It seems to me, you had to be wildly in love or you weren't alive . . . excuse me, when you were young. Sooooo"— she scratched her ear for no reason at all, and she knew it—"anyone who would be foolish enough to marry you, had to know what happened, had to make believe he was either a medical student or an English pilot or both!"

"Both, and then some," I said. "An impossible dreamer, a fighter, a changer, an itchy reformer, a sentimental fool who can sing every love song I ever wrote and forgot, but not he; a life-on-the-line idealist, a courtly, patient, passionate, loving man, but he never learned to tango! You know that, Willow."

Jules's key was in the door, and she went running.

DECLINING
YEARS

Willow Wizens/ The Pacemaker

WATCHING Willow and Kelly together in her declining years was proof that nothing was impossible.

More to interest herself than to teach him, she put him through endless lectures on the Great Books. In her delicate but firm style, she pontificated about the ways of higher mammal behavior hidden under all those clothes. Tattered or satin, the search was the same—how to get out of ugly into beauty, and in the final analysis (that was becoming one of her favorite phrases), nothing was ugly if you were a student of life. You'll never be a writer the way I am, dear heart, little bastard, she told him, but I'll tell you anyway. It all ends in death, after all. But you haven't the faintest notion about what I'm saying, have you?

Kelly almost did, with great effort, but made believe he didn't, to let her feel exceptional.

Their first few years together, Willow wore a clothespin on her nose whenever Kelly got too close, to remind him of his less-endowed, second-place, inferior genes.

They lived together for ten years. In her old age, Willow fought deafness, and despite her grudging stance, she had to admit that Kelly was a dear boon, telling her when dinner was ready; she couldn't hear the plates being put down anymore, or the bells ringing to announce guests, or our voices. No more cooing or yelling, only eye contact, faces close, lip-reading. Curiously, she still did her somersaults and tried to teach him that crazy exaltation, but decided he wasn't smart enough, or his soul wasn't amused and sophisticated enough to break into "Singin' in the Rain." There was a pragmatic, a staunch burgher citizen thing about Kelly, an absence of giggle; he was all sturdy wool, cowlicks and scratchy trousers. But he did pick up some of Willow's tricks, and she was as pleased as an old lady handing over her favorite down-home recipes: Throw an ashtray off a table when you're hungry, bang on the kitchen cabinet with the loose hinges, it makes more noise when you want a sweet; demand breakfast at six, throw your body against a door by seven if there is no reaction. Be tolerant when they make love; don't intrude on that, but when it's over, demand a cookie.

In her last years she permitted him to wash her ears (just a minute or so, no more!) with little licks of affection, to get the dust out; she was too weary to do it herself. Poor little peasant, Kelly had tried for years to sleep next to her, lean on her for a cozy snooze, but she would have none of it . . . not until she felt so cold all the time. Even she had to admit that she had gotten used to his bobbity male smell. She needed him. His proximity was comforting. Old age needed to be revered, and Kelly was there to do it. If pushed to it, she might even have admitted that Kelly kept her going. *That* was a truth. What courage to admit a truth. Particularly when it had to do with honoring others and the ways of loving.

You could see she spent most of her time thinking, and getting smaller and smaller with each question, almost as if she were imploding into herself like a very distant star.

Miss Willow wizened. Old age meant shrinking. She was sleeping around the clock. Oh, still eating . . . too well, too voraciously, like a condemned one defying fate; yet her body got nothing from the eating. She was shrinking by the day.

Willow wasn't the only one who was shrinking and aging around us. The others were in a suburb of Boston—my aunt and uncle. He was ninety-two and she was in her late eighties, but she looked like a healthy seventy-five and didn't deny it. She was still a woman of lingering beauty and agility; only her brain sometimes worked in the teeter-totter rhythms of the aged—that avalanche of memory, experience, youth, and dream flooding the Present at any given moment, to make a Now filled with the Furies.

Uncle Zachariah was my mother's "baby brother," the black sheep of his family, and he had outlived them all, with his wit, evasive spirit, and artist's soul.

I was his *nearest* niece in affection, though I didn't deserve to be, because we didn't see one another for years at a time. But our habit *was* to talk on the phone. He would call: "I just wanted to find out how your life is. . . ." Notice, it wasn't "How are you?" It had to be philosophical or his patience ran out. It was required that I talk fast, or before I knew it he was saying "Good-bye. Your Aunt Ponia sends you her love."

The dreaded phone call came one day, from the wife of their landlord. My uncle had had a heart attack and was in the hospital. My aunt wanted me to know; she couldn't call herself because she was deaf. Yes, I know that, I said. Would the caller (who sounded affectionate and concerned for both old people) please get the name of the doctor in charge of my uncle and call me back?

The doctor told me they were planning to put a pacemaker into my ninety-two-year-old uncle because that's what he wanted. He wasn't ready to die yet, it didn't fit in with his plans. If he died, then that was fate. If he didn't? Then he had a few more years of dream. "That's what he said," the doctor reported, "so we'll take the chance of his not making it on the table." "He's alert?" I asked. "Clear as a bell. The Fire Department got to him very fast and started his heart up; there wasn't much oxygen loss."

I was in Boston by late afternoon. Who else but me? And I hated hospitals, I reeled in them. Bad things happened in hospitals, especially large city ones filled with sadness, the anger of the overworked staff and the doctors who developed acres of scar tissue against involvement. There were cousins who lived in the next town who had been most thoughtful of my aunt and uncle for years, dropping in for visits, keeping a watchful eye. But if death were near, who else should keep vigil but the favorite niece who hadn't been thoughtful, who only called on the telephone?

Aunt Ponia had just had tea and was clearing away the kitchen table. "May I help you?" I asked in a loud voice, remembering her deafness. "No, sit down, you just traveled," she said.

"Not much. It's just an hour away by plane—"

I wasn't sure she heard, but out it came like a bolt. "Why couldn't you come when he was well? Too far away? He's been waiting for you for years. Now he isn't here." She mumbled to herself, "I know you people, you go to the country to visit trees, but you can't come to see your uncle."

I felt painted with guilt shellac from head to toe.

And then she began talking nonstop for two days.

Out poured a marriage of sixty years, the love, the hate, the everything a woman can feel who had straddled two centuries and loved the most difficult man who had ever lived in any century. My aunt was a trained nurse and had helped support my uncle and herself for years. "He was my most difficult patient, I nursed him for sixty years, your Uncle Stubborn. He used to like to wear hats, all kinds of hats, he was like a street urchin when I met him; he never knew how to dress, how to do anything. I married a philosopher."

The apartment was scrupulously clean.

Pride of place outweighed the drab, the tiny income of the elderly. It was replete with artistic choices, objects invested with sentiment, books, paintings (my uncle owned a tiny Sisley!), a handsome samovar, a faded but fine Oriental rug. Begonia plants covered the windowsills of the living room, and there were crisp, white doilies and lace antimacassars on the furniture. She had her rocker; he had his battered wing chair. There was a large maple tree growing outside, and somehow the presence of light was very active in the little place, filtering through the sheer white curtains.

"I knew he wasn't feeling well . . . he eats raisin bread in warm milk only when he doesn't feel good. 'What's wrong, Zachariah?' I said. 'Nothing, don't worry, I'm feeling weak. Maybe I'm just having an identity crisis, like everyone else. Pretty soon I'll have the opportunity for a deep analysis with Freud himself. Stop worrying,' he said. I told him: 'Stop fooling, I'm going to call the doctor.' He wouldn't let me. 'What are you except weak?' I insisted. 'I'm ninety-two, that's what I am,' he tells me. 'Who I am is something else. I don't know, do you?'

he says to me. Oh, your uncle . . . Then he asks me to get into bed with him in the middle of the afternoon. Was he crazy altogether? When a person isn't feeling well, one person in a twin bed is enough. Then he said we should call you, he didn't talk to you for a long time."

She sighed. "If I did call the doctor, what could I tell him? That my husband was weak, he ate raisin bread in warm milk, he wanted me to get into bed with him, and he wants to talk to a niece he never sees? The doctor would think I'm not responsible!"

She had to tell me over and over how it happened. It was dawn, and he must have gotten up to go to the bathroom, where they always kept the light on, it was her rule—no tripping. She didn't hear him. How could she, with her ears? He must have fallen. The birds were very loud, so she knew it was dawn. He wasn't in his bed. (She could hear the birds?) She found him lying between the toilet and the sink, she said, with not a pulse. "No pulse!" She kept repeating the terror of the scene: "Help! Help! My husband has fainted, he's dying! Call the Fire Department!" She then banged on the walls, and the neighbors came running, she said, adding, "You know, even if we're Jews, they're very friendly; your uncle is much appreciated." (I thought: My God, was it true, on a little working-class street in a suburb of Boston, was her feeling real—about being Jewish—or was it the baggage of a lifetime?)

I lit a cigarette. "Don't smoke!" she ordered. "I inhale it, and it makes me nervous. Give it up. He had to give it up. He loved to smoke, millions of cigars, for years. Can you imagine how many cigars a man can smoke if he's ninety-two and he gave them up when he was eighty-eight? He supported Cuba for most of his life! He also supported Scotland, your magnanimous uncle with his shot glasses of whiskey. 'What do you need a fire in your throat for all the time?' I asked him. 'Join the circus and become a real fire-eater. At least you'll be paid for it.'" She looked at me. "Cigars and liquor ruined his health."

I'd settle for ninety-two years of ruination, I said to myself.

"Oh, I'm so glad you're here, I have you all to myself. Remember how I used to sing to you, 'Mary, Mary, quite contrary'? And you were . . . a contrary little girl, but we loved you, with your thin little face and black bangs over your green eyes. You were a delicious little child, I could eat you up. . . ."

The jump in years was making me dizzy, and I couldn't smoke, and she was hard of hearing, and I had to yell. It *was just too much.* I *had* to tell her about the pacemaker, prepare her, but I couldn't get a word in that she didn't control.

"You came to answer the phone because I can't hear if the doctors call . . ."

"I also came to be with you . . ."

"I've taken care of myself my whole life, I've never asked anyone for help. What's wrong with him? He'll rest up for a few days and he'll be fine, poor man. I know my patient; they don't know him. They don't know he likes sardines and onions for lunch. No, that's not right, is it? I'm trying to take the clock by the throat and make it change its mind. He's a very sick man, isn't he? He fainted away . . ."

"No, it was heart failure, Aunt Ponia."

"Ah, heart failure . . . of course, a faint heart . . . from old age. What can you expect? I'll have to get used to it." Her hands

flew to her face. "Why couldn't I have antic-
ipated it? I'm falling down on the job. No, I
must be steady as a gyroscope. . . ." She
clapped her hands together like a child. "We
never came or went against each other. People get restless, they go out looking and trying for something new, crossing paths that
shouldn't be crossed, getting lost. Not us. We
started together and stayed. We experi-
mented on each other, always like this"—she
showed me her clasped hands and began
to sing a little plaint of delight: " 'Yes, sir,
he's my baby, no, sir, I don't mean
maybe . . .' "

Gyroscope? You old sea dog! You're incredible, I said to myself. She had disappeared into the bathroom and there were
sounds of objects being moved. She stuck her
head out the door. "Are you very fancy? I'm
making room for your toilet articles. Your
mother hated perfume. Do you like it?"

"I love it!" I said.

"I just have one bottle," she responded.
L'Heure Bleu . . . the same smell for years.
Your uncle's brother, Isadore, *the rich one,*
brought it back to me from Paris once. A
huge bottle. He never bought anything but

huge. It lasted forever. Then I bought my own, I was so used to it. Why make yourself nervous choosing something new—I like it, I don't like it—Blue Hour suits me." She disappeared into the bathroom again, talking nonetheless. "I use Oil of Olay and wipe it off with cotton balls." She was giggling. "I'm an advanced student of the magazines."

There she was, wiping her face with a cotton ball, laughing. "At my age, I'm still running after the wrinkles. There was a time when they ran after me."

She pointed to the begonia windows. "How do you like my tree out there? It was dying when we moved here, the landlord was ready to cut it down. 'No, no,' I said, 'I'll sit under it and talk to it.' Don't laugh, it accommodated me because it knew I loved it. Look how beautiful it is today . . . it's *my* tree. You look like my voice is bothering you; I can't help it. Deaf people have to hear themselves in the throat, you'll just have to stand it. . . .

"Did you know your uncle went to a college to study architecture when he was young?" I registered surprise. "He ran away from college, *he* had to learn from the air.

. . ." She saw a look of complicity on my face. "You understand that?"

I articulated it carefully: "Very well!"

"How can you be an architect from the air? He should never have ended up a brick-layer; it ruined his back. He was too sensitive to be a workman, but what could he do? He had no trade. Playing chess, writing poems is not a trade. Ah, he got me with his poems."

"I didn't know he wrote poems. . . ."

"Go to the library, ask for his poems, and you'll see! He had crazy friends, too, all around us when we were young. There was Dada, you know? A painter named Burliuk, what a crazy man he was; he used to walk in the street with flowers painted on his face and who knew where else. . . . Dada, Mama, such naughtiness, tear down the old, up with the new, they were all crazy, including your uncle, the bricklayer who wrote po-etry. And I was an intelligent, pretty nurse, that's what he got! He ran after me, he grabbed what he wanted, he wouldn't take no for an answer. What did I want with mar-riage? I wanted to be a doctor. I've taken good care of him, my patient for sixty years, with his allergies, his bronchitis, his every-thing."

The late sun was streaming through the white, sheer curtains. "See? We watch the sunset every day. We love the light through the curtains. It's a nice little apartment, isn't it? The sun in the east, for breakfast; in the west, for supper." She had a private, languid look. "I gave in to him!" The look turned to anger. "I relinquished my future for him! I sold myself into slavery!"

Nothing was going to stop her; she needed me to know and share—the demand was in her eyes. "You babies now, you know nothing about terrible times. In my village in Russia, there were no schools, only a red hut with a teacher for the Gentile children. You know what my mother did? She gave the teacher money secretly, to teach my brother on our back steps. I insisted it was for me, too, and I learned. A girl! My brother came to America and became a doctor. I could have done the same, I had the kind of brain that reached in and took like a hummingbird from a flower." She made herself tremble, imitating the wings of a bird. "Yes, I would have made a fine doctor, but he wouldn't let me. And I listened to him."

I dared to come to my uncle's defense: "It wasn't his fault that you listened to him."

"What's the matter with you? Don't you know the history of feminism?" It was said with such a rush of feeling, I didn't know whether to laugh or cry for the book she had flung open. Neither. She was like a newly washed window reeking with ammonia and gleaming in the sun.

"I'm a nineteenth-century woman," she said, proud of the time she had managed to span. "A few of us slipped through the net, we became nurses, secretaries; a few exceptional ones, doctors, lawyers. Ah . . . it would take a long Russian short story to explain why I listened to him."

I wanted to hug her, but that wasn't what we did in our family. Or hadn't. "You've been a reader all your life . . ." I offered as a compliment or a balm, but she took it as neither.

"Of course! A human being reads! If you're a chipmunk, you don't read!" She drew in a breath. "Those were terrible, different times. Do you know what it means to be so ambitious, to be filled with so many sparks, they fly out of your eyes? *That* was your Aunt Ponia. What possessed me not to do what I wanted? Those terrible times for a woman? Love? Did I want him so much?" she asked with a single laugh. "I must have. Anyway, he threatened me, he said if I didn't marry him, he'd commit suicide. He was very handsome, my dear philosopher." She began to cry and had to sit down. Suddenly she was her true eighty-eight years, a browning, shaking fern, exhausted and root-bound.

She had made me heavy with her lost dreams, her choices made. It obviously never stopped, the unresolved, the unconscious (uninvited) coming out of the fog, disappearing into it, and cleverly calling itself fate when the spoon of history stirred it. She was telling me something without knowing she was telling me: "Seize time!"

I drew her to the couch under the begonia windows. I had to explain to her about the pacemaker and that I would take her to the hospital the next afternoon. I sat close and talked loudly, but she refused to understand.

A pacemaker? What is it, a harness, a breast-plate, inside, outside? They didn't have such things when she was nursing. In him? On him? I tried to explain that it was to control the beat of his heart.

"Or he will die," she said, yet went on as if she hadn't said it. "It's an operation! He'll never allow it. I'll never give my permission. It's up to him and he won't agree." I tried to interrupt, to tell her I'd spoken with the doctor and my uncle had agreed, but she wasn't listening.

"He's too frightened of operations, I know." She began to whisper. "He had such trouble with his prostate. Not unusual for old men, but for him it was a Greek tragedy. That's when we got our twin beds. He wouldn't let them operate, he studied and he talked to six doctors and he found out, he said, almost every dead old man on the autopsy table had cancer of the prostate, and he didn't even know it, and that's *not* why he died. He said he was going to be one of those old men and his prostate would be a mystery until he died, and not even then, because he would divorce me if I permitted an autopsy, since he was going first. Why would I want an autopsy for him? I told him he was crazy. All right, the doctor said to him, if that's the way you want it, but it wouldn't be good to have *intercourse,*" she whispered her whisper. "It can cause bleeding . . . so we haven't tried for years. We hold each other. . . . No, he'll never allow an operation; he'd rather slip away."

Desperate to be understood, I insisted she listen and hear that I had talked with the doctor and that Uncle Zachariah had given his permission.

She looked at me suspiciously and started to berate me. "It's you who brought that word 'pacemaker' into this house. It's nobody's business but my husband's. Not you! Not me!"

I yelled: "You're refusing to listen, damn it! He gave his permission, he signed the release!"

With maddening calm, she responded, "Ah . . . he did? You see? He wants to live. He doesn't want to leave me." Her eyes filled up, and a few tears rolled down her soft, pretty cheeks. I put my arms around her and suggested she lie down to rest. "Maybe I will," she said. "You've seen too much al-

ready. I feel like a cracked cup for the first
time in my life, and it isn't good to leak
yourself out, it isn't healthy." She straightened her back, looking for the plumb line of
youth, and amazingly seemed younger in
front of my eyes.

She prepared our supper and wouldn't let
me help; I was only to sit at the maple table
with its ladderback chairs and watch. I listened! Did I know my uncle had an art gallery when they were young? (I had heard
some vague family stories, but said no, I
didn't.) "Oh, did he run an art gallery," she
said. "Gallery for the People, he called it, in
the ghetto of Boston. Paintings and paintings. He also had a friend, Henry Miller, a
writer who made watercolors because he
needed money."

"Henry Miller who wrote *Tropic of Cancer?*" I asked.

She was impatient with me—was there
any other? "He gave your uncle a roll of
drawings to sell, and the greenhorns came to
look. But they didn't have money to buy
laundry soap. How could they buy paintings?" she challenged. "What happened? Everyone went home with a watercolor as a

present, and Henry Miller was so furious he never talked to your uncle again. Did you ever hear of such a thing? How can you run a business when you give away the merchandise?" she dared me to answer.

How brave she was trying to be, though totally exhausted and drained, apprehensive and fragile. Still I was not to help. I came to help my uncle, not her, she said.

There was little in the refrigerator but cold, ancient chicken, she apologized. I would have to excuse her, the time was not normal. But wait until morning, *that* she had, and would she make me a wonderful breakfast!

As we sat at the table, both trying to swallow a kind of supper, she kept looking at me. "I had to teach you to eat when you were a little girl." The loving timbre in "little girl" touched me so strangely I had to look away. "Do you remember?" she asked. "Your mother couldn't make you eat, so she used to send you to me, because I always did special things for you. And your Uncle Zachariah would tell you wonderful stories while you ate. He made believe he was telling them to me; you're not supposed to seduce a child to eat. Oh, the fairy tales that rolled out of his mouth for you. And how you listened, and how you ate while you listened!" Her eyes were twinkling and she clapped her hands with delight.

I went to the sink counter to sneak up on helping her do the dishes, and she suddenly turned on me: "Here! Get away! You don't know how to do my dishes! I told you no!" She snatched the dishcloth out of my hand.

"I'm a big girl, Aunt Ponia, I do dishes very well. I'm a good housekeeper. For heaven's sake, I want to help."

She pushed me aside roughly. "I do them like this, and like this, you don't know my way!" She slammed the dishes about to show me *her way,* and she gave me a shove.

"Stop it!"

"You're disturbing my system. Don't you know about order? It must be respected!" She had come so close, I had a horrible feeling she was going to strike me. I turned my back.

"I'm a calm person," she said. "You're the opposite, like your uncle. I don't like you to agitate me. You think you can help me?" A deep, robust, cynical laugh came out of her.

"*My* mother taught us to do well under any conditions. *Your* mother didn't teach you to behave properly. Your mother! She was too busy filling her head with Santayana, Thomas Mann, Freud, Marx! She didn't know whether she was coming or going, and neither did they when it came to loving a child. Only ideas! There is such a thing as protocol. You are in *my* house. You're not good for me. . . ."

My fury got the best of my fascination with hearing the testimony of a live witness to my childhood. Slow, soft, and nasty, I said: "You didn't like her, did you? Tell me about my mother. I don't remember her, except in the pit of my stomach."

The old lady blanched.

"Did I miss much not knowing her. *You* tell me. There's no one else left to tell me, except . . . Uncle Zachariah, and he—"

She burst into tears. "No, no. What's wrong with you? Don't say such things, I loved her."

"You heard every word I said, didn't you!"

"Stop it, you naughty girl. Your mother was a brilliant, beautiful woman. Stop it, I'm not used to company . . . my balance is falling away. What am I going to do if he doesn't come home?"

I was filled with remorse.

I slept in my uncle's twin bed next to hers that night. She had excused herself after the blowup, went to sleep immediately, and *I* did the dishes, sat in the living room smoking, and was sure I would not sleep a wink in their bedroom, sure she would have the windows closed—the enemy of old bones was a night draft. My nose would get all stuffed from breathing in age and the smell of endings. The quiet in their apartment was making my ears ring. I couldn't remember who I was, whether I was five or forty-five. Jules's wife? Chuck's mother? Or the little girl.

Breakfast was all ready when I woke. She was wearing a pink housecoat and looked like a strawberry ice cream cone. I snuck up behind her and gave her a kiss. She loved the morning, she said, it was wonderful to have another beginning as usual, just wait, I would find out for myself one day. She hoped I didn't mind the open windows at night, she didn't approve of sleeping in an

airless room, because cobwebs grew, an un-
pleasant smell. She complimented me on the
way I slept . . . "quietly, with your head in
the middle of the pillow. Your uncle thrashes
around, he makes big waves with his bed-
clothes, and I'm awakened by a hurricane.
He doesn't like my hospital corners; he says
his legs are anarchists."

I had to eat every bit of the breakfast she
made "just the way I do for your uncle. He
loves his hot cereal with the sweet pat of
butter sitting on top like a little sun . . .
and oh, how he loves his coffee." She began
to laugh. "He calls it his 'muddy fountain of
youth'; it reminds his brain to be young."

I arranged that a taxi would bring us to
the hospital by noon. The operation would
be over by then and he would be back in the
intensive-care unit, just in case he was in
trouble.

We both became very busy cleaning up
and getting dressed. She let me help her clear
the table and complimented me on the way I
had done the dishes the night before. When I
was in the bathroom she yelled out: "Have
you moved your bowels?" I yelled back
"No!" She answered: "Isn't it amazing how

the bowels are connected to the head? Everything is connected to the head, it's the secret
of nursing to know that. Can you imagine
how upset the entire country must be, with
so many advertisements to help the bowels?"
She heard me laughing in the bathroom.
"Your uncle says, when they stop those com-
mercials for headaches, piles, and constipa-
tion, then we'll know that democracy in
America is successful." I came out laughing,
but she was silent and looked at me. "I don't
want to live if he doesn't. There would be no
point to my time. And who would hire an
old nurse? Shakespeare, for his Juliet! Who
else?" Her morning humor returned, with a
sad little shake of its tail.

"I always loved your smile," I said, and
kissed her. "Your job is just to be calm today. Everything will be fine, and we must be
quiet as mice in the hospital." She understood what I meant—that talking loudly because of her deafness wouldn't be right in the
ICU, we'd wake people out of their comas.
"Maybe we should," she said.

She was all dressed long before I was, and
ready to go. "How do you like my Hong
Kong suit?" she asked, turning stylishly. "I

bought it years ago. Everyone was buying Hong Kong suits. Why not me? Today it's not special, nothing is made in America. But I always sew lace on my collars, it keeps them clean. Old-fashioned but nice. Don't you agree? Your uncle likes the way I dress." She paused. "One thing he does know, and that's his art. I knew my nursing and he knew his art. He couldn't have managed without my nursing, with his allergies, his bronchitis, his God knows what." She paused again. "Maybe I couldn't have managed without his art."

She was trying to put on her pearls, but her fingers were trembling and she had a distant look in her eyes. "They used to call me the angel of death when I was nursing in the hospital. They gave me the most difficult cases. The person who was dying always went quietly when I sat next to them, just turning the head to the side, going with a soft sigh. . . . What a blessing it is to die quietly. They used to say, 'It only happens that way when Ponia is in the room.'

"Can you help me with my pearls? I can't manage the clasp." I came to help her. "I sat with your mother for three days before she died."

I pulled away as if I had been touched by a live wire. "I didn't know you were there! I didn't know anything! They didn't tell me she was dying . . . they thought I was too young." I began to cry hysterically, mostly from the shock of still being vulnerable to such ancient history. She drew me to the couch under the begonia windows and held me in her arms.

"Now, now, don't cry, little one. See how nice it is to have a woman hold you sometimes, isn't it? No matter how old you are. It doesn't have to be a mother, just a woman holding another woman." She kept patting my back until the tears stopped.

"I don't believe in anything but life," she cooed. "I haven't played any games with God—I believe in you, I don't believe in you. I'm not frightened, I don't believe in anything but life. If I cry, it's not from fear. Only from imagining loneliness. My tears are because life is such a gift, so short, and no one knows who sent it."

I got up to get away from the nearness, and picked up the pearls from the floor. I had come to help her, not to have her help me. She stood up, straight and strong. "Don't worry about me," she said. "I'll be fine, there's more than one devil in me yet." And she laughed. "You're getting to feel familiar, you're like your uncle, high-strung and nervous. Oh, what a family . . ."

I clasped the pearls for her and went into the bathroom to pull myself together. A closed door didn't mean I couldn't hear her, and she knew it.

"Sometimes I wish I were just a little doggie. It's so simple: just to be a dog. Just to eat, sleep, chew a bone, bark, lift your leg against a wall while you're going somewhere." She was laughing quietly to herself.

I opened the bathroom door and saw her leaning forward, talking to an imagined animal. "Tell me, little doggie, what is it to be simply human? *You* know who you are! You are a doggie. Your head doesn't have to be philosophical, your heart doesn't have to feel tragedy and love."

Uncle Zachariah had survived the pacemaker implant very well. Aunt Ponia sat quiet as a mouse while he and I talked. He was very happy to see me, but why under such circumstances? He said he couldn't stand where he was, it was full of old and dying people. And he felt positively surreal, and it wasn't his favorite style of painting. He said it was a problem when you outlive everyone; the canvas you were painted on is no more, you're without a background, a frame, even. I kept looking over at my Aunt Ponia, who had a little closed smile on her face, as if to say, "That's your uncle. Did you ever hear of anyone talking like that after an operation? He's crazy. . . ." Yes, quite wonderfully mad. And leave it to him to have a pregnant nurse, who came in to check on the monitors and everything else he was hitched up to.

"The twenty-first century she has in her," he said. "And here I am, half here, half there, suspended, like I'm leaning against a Dali clock. I tell you, with this thing inside me, this pacemaker going tick-tick and I can't even hear it because it doesn't *have* a tick-tick . . . maybe that's what happened to me, *I am the Dali clock!* Don't hang around here, go home and work," he told me. "Maybe you'll even write down somewhere that I was your uncle."

When we got back to the apartment, Aunt Ponia was euphoric. His color was good, she said; he looked like a prince, didn't he? She had to have the pacemaker explained to her again. He'd be the same, only better? The pacemaker would last from three to seven years before it had to be changed? Then what would happen when he was ninety-nine? Science would find another what? Another miracle?

"By then both of us will be an endangered species, a miracle of love!" she exclaimed.

I suppressed a smile.

"You're laughing at me?"

She began to laugh. "I'm laughing at myself, too."

The trauma of it was too much. He couldn't recover from the onslaught of the catheter, the implant of a pacemaker. It worked too well. The pacemaker, not he, hung on beyond all reason. He was so interested in words. He had said once, years before, on the telephone, that *reason* was a word tree nymphs used only on a summer afternoon, after a Dionysian rite; human beings didn't know the word *reason*.

Uncle Zachariah came home from the hospital, incontinent and in diapers. There was no *reason* to that, and he died not long after. Which was a very wise decision on his part. I'm certain it was his decision.

Yet, the pacemaker had given us a last chance to visit. On my way to the airport the next day after the operation, I saw him without Aunt Ponia. He took that opportunity to tell me he didn't have money to leave me, but he *did* have something, maybe more valuable. It was what he had observed very early, when I was little. "Myself, I was a total failure," he said. "So it made me a better judge of imperfections. She made terrible mistakes with you, your mother. You know, she was the love of my life. Think how your Aunt Ponia felt about that. . . . Yes, my sister's biggest mistake was to die so young, not to be able to make it up, to sit with you, two grown people eye to eye. I think she could have done it if she'd lived; I know she could. Her problem was that she thought she was the field commander of a battalion of potential angels—you and your sister."

I couldn't believe what was happening. Not one of my elders had ever spoken of *what went on,* or feelings. Not one.

He told me that I wasn't wrong, I *had* been "emotionally battered," and he hoped I would forgive them (my parents).

Why didn't he come to my aid? I asked. It would have saved me fifty thousand dollars! I accused as angrily as I could allow in an ICU unit. "Me?" he said. "Me, the black sheep? They put away the silver when I came," he joked. "I played chess, horses, wrote poems, I had a good time. You can't trust the word of someone who has a good time."

After he died, I was filled with lectures to myself. When he was here, I wasn't. It was comfortable to be absent. There never was time to take a couple of days off to visit an aging uncle. Now, there was no one left to be harangued by, no one to minister to, be ministered by—as only family can do and be done to. That intruding, necessary love— family; that tie to blood and bone, nature's belonging, even to the dishonorable that is yours. And he had gracefully stayed away, except on the telephone, because that is what he had been, in his sister's eyes, he thought: dishonorable. It was too late to beg to differ with him. Mama had always said his name in a very special way.

I was going to miss his crooked ray of sun, sporadic but intense over the years, and finally, weak and late, as it touched me.

He was buried near my mother and father's grave, in Peabody. The cemetery is on a hill, with a view. There were a few nieces, cousins, an old friend of Uncle Zachariah's from the old Gallery for the People days, who was pushing ninety-two himself. Aunt Ponia was amazing, wearing a simple black dress as elegant as a Balenciaga, with one string of pearls and a small diamond cluster on her shoulder, and walking firmly, with the small smile of the seasoned hostess. Aunt Ponia died within the year. After her burial, attended by the same relatives and friends, we had a party for her. Two parties in a year, for people who never saw each other! We had smoked salmon, cream cheese, a bowl of green grapes, a starched white tablecloth—

what Zachariah would have wanted, I thought, if he had outlived her. And I had L'Heure Bleu, Blue Hour, splashed all over me, the last of her bottle.

A New Kind of Love

WHAT *is* infinity? I asked a mathematician once, at a party. What else do you ask a man who spends his life with numbers and has just finished two martinis? Exploit him while he's vulnerable; you want something from him he'd never give sober.

"That which goes on forever," he had chortled patiently. "But anything that goes on forever is irrational, so infinity is described by irrational numbers, meaning we don't know."

"Aren't numbers supposed to lead to certainty?"

"Numbers should lead to certainty, not

uncertainty, but numbers can *only* lead to uncertainty," he said and cast anxious eyes about the room, looking for his wife. (He wasn't drunk enough.)

I was drunk enough (on grief and tonic) when I got back from my uncle's funeral to want to find infinity in the corner of my eye —that is, stop the clock. Then everything would stay as it was, *forever.* Willow would not wizen and shrink, I would not move into the future that was inevitable: old age. Jules would not leave me first, according to the insurance companies' actuarial tables. I had already warned him that if he died, I would just close the door of the apartment and leave; I could never orchestrate his funeral, he'd be on his own until the police rammed the door down because a neighbor smelled *something.* I would be far away, because I would not be able to deal with his death. In that case, Jules said, he would certainly make it his business not to die first.

Stop the clock: Chuck would remain Chucky; my nephew Peter's receding hairline, inherited from my father and his father, would come to a halt. Kelly would remain a capsule for sweetness in perpetuity.

"What's wrong with you," Jules said, "is that you've lost your last elder. Their book is closed. *We* are now the elders!"

"You mean filled with wisdom and deep laughter?" I mocked, even as I wished it could be true.

"If not now, when?"

"But I'm just learning how to tie my own shoelaces!"

" 'Grow old along with me, the best is yet to be. . . .' "

"Robert Browning was only forty-two when he wrote that, and he didn't have grandchildren. If he did, it might have been: Grow old and young with me, the most revealing and exhausting are yet to be."

Chucky had become Chuck. He had gone to college and graduate school, married a blond temptress (the eternal usurper of sons, according to all mothers) who was completing her doctorate, who would become a professor, a genius juggler of time—*the new woman.* They would have one son, and another little creature was swimming about in the amniotic fluid. One and one equal three and a half, equal certainty *and* infinity both. Grandchildren: the mathematics of continuity and the perpetual balance wheel! A new kind of love. If you didn't know who you were, you'd better learn immediately or fake magnificently. Because new eyes are watching, not to judge, but *only* for learning and loving, wisdom and deep laughter.

"Do you know what the sun is?" little Ben asks, his hand in mine, while showing me his secret path through the garden.

"Of course! Isn't it a wonder? Let me tell you all about the sun," I said, in the wise and steady voice of a shaman. (Maybe I could do it better this second chance around. I wasn't, after all, a young, nervous mother with her firstborn. Wasn't I an elder whose only job was to protect and defend the wonders?)

Ben had felt familiar from the minute he was born, a tiny, premature infant lying in an incubator, with gauze across his eyes. The first word he said was "light." I feared for him; he would always be looking for *light,* never be satisfied unless he understood that its absence, sometimes, was not his doing. I predicted, in my heart, that this child would always be both trembling and strong. It was there in him, from the beginning, the eyes that sensed all, a nervous system that could shake with anger when perfection was denied. (Elizabeth all over again, but with parents, thank God, who could be playful, loving, urge him into his strengths, let him fashion himself, use his trembling, searching spirit as *he* wished, not as *they* wished.)

I looked at Ben and knew this, and he knew I knew his signals: Oh, how they do come and go, especially her, my working mother, my one, my own, my dearest. When she leaves the room, the world leaves with her. Is there a shadow of criticism in my new flashing thoughts? Well, not criticism, just questions. . . . The thing I want most is sameness, because everything is so exciting, exhausting, sometimes even terrifying. Yes, what I want is sameness, day after day, for even in the calmness, every minute is a new explosion of learning. Rub my spine, someone, I'm having a fit of learning!

"He's willful," say the new, young, harried parents in the changing, two-parent-working world, rushing from baby-sitter orders to job, to shopping, to driving, to home, to loving, to bedtime stories, to late-night study, to exhaustion, to begin again in the morning.

"Of course he's willful, a possessor of will! Sharp and fine as a champion colt-to-be; every normal child is."

"How to tame him? Let him know he can't manipulate?"

"Send him to a sergeant in the Marine Corps!" said the shaman. "If you want him to be without will!"

Define *civilized*. What shall we say to him who has all the tongues within him? Do we honor his eyes while we train his computing brain? Do we count on his microscopic watching as he watches us pass on what was handed down to us? Or is he new, to climb an unscaled peak, to breathe an unbreathed breath so far? "Don't touch the hot!" snorts the old shaman. That's easy. Of course we teach him his skin needs saving! But then what? Maybe we should simply be, for him to watch. Be what? What a test. Imagine watching us, our eyes, mouths, walk, talk, kiss, touch; imagine watching us expand, contract, explode, ignore; or if we celebrate or kill. We must look into his eyes. They'll tell us who we are."

"You know, you better watch your step," Willow said. "When the kids are here, you're impossible; that's all you do is criticize."

The little wizened lady, much to our surprise, enjoyed having Ben around. She allowed his tweaks and squeezes and deftly got out of his way, not running off to hide, just meowing a warning and he understood. We explained to Ben that Willow was as old as Father Time, and he respected that completely. Chuck was already a *boy* when Willow came to live with us. She knew dirty sneakers but she had never known a human baby. She was fascinated and indulgent, and obviously, from what I was hearing, critical of me in the situation.

"Are you telling me that I should keep my mouth shut?"

"Yes! If the boy"—she still called Chuck "the boy" . . . as I did too, in my head!— "weren't so good-natured and loving with you and Him, maybe you wouldn't see them as much as you'd like."

"He values my opinion," I protested.

"Don't push it. Forewarned is fore-armed," she said.

"Where did you get that idea?"

"Picking up the other side of your thoughts, the you-know-when-you're-guilty ones."

"I want to be perfect. It's a terrible world out there."

The minute I heard myself say it, I remembered something Uncle Zachariah had once expressed in one of our long telephone calls together, to remind me that *his* generation was significantly better than mine. (Was it ever thus?)

"Next to us," he said, "your hippies and yippies who turned into the allrightniks when they hit thirty, were babies sucking their thumbs." ("Yuppie" wasn't invented yet, or he would have relished using it, I'm sure.) "It was a monumental wildness when we were young. Grand. We came to America like ponies breathing fire. The Atlantic Ocean was the highway to the magic land of Indian feathers and Thomas Paine. We had ideals, our names were written in some holy book, we thought. We brought our Tolstoy and our Rousseau and Voltaire, our music

and poems. Dirty foreigners. Royalty in
rags. We were bursting, but not for ourselves, for ideas, books, humanity. We turned
America upside down, with our strikes, our
unions . . . who ever heard of unions before the immigrants came? It was all the
fault of Thomas Jefferson. He got something
into his head about 'life, liberty, and the pursuit of happiness,' and we took him seri-
ously."

What else could I say but, "You're
right!"?

Could I say to Chuck and Sandy, "It was
a grand wildness when we were young, you
babies, we did it better, more sensitively, we,
the Freudian, romantic generation?" I'd better not! Willow was right. I'd make them feel
as resentful as I did listening to *my* elder,
even if I adored him. My uncle's generation
was probably the last to *dare* to say proudly,
"Look what we've done!"

My generation invented the atomic bomb
and used it. But maybe we forced our foolish
species to have apocolyptic second thoughts
about the meaning of what Willow called the
Absolute Peaceful Hand, by discovering Its
final warning: It's not so clever to be so

clever in the Garden, or there'll be no Garden!

It would eventually come to pass that we have four grandchildren: Benjamin, Daniel, Joshua, and Rachel. Willow would only know Benjamin.

"What are you doing, creating a new biblical dynasty?" we ask.

The answer was, "Why not? Isn't it time?"

Again I am of two minds. More births, into this world of overpopulation and hunger? Yet I can now understand and feel in my soul the multiplication table, the command "Go forth and multiply." It doesn't simply mean "Lie down, hopefully in bliss, and copulate." It means two parents, four grandparents, eight great-grandparents, back, back to the beginning, to the slow roll of genes perfecting, imprinting, collecting endless memories of places and peoples, eyes, spirits, characteristics, quirks, looks, loves, talents, madnesses, a glorious, luscious gathering of genes . . . and forward to, at least, the *human* concept of infinity. I am infinitely, viscerally connected, fatally bound to the middle, between past and present, between what was and what will be. My genes will whirl into space in four different ways, have four different chances to realize the universe.

I have been made an elder! And wise. I know how many dragonflies it takes to sink a floating leaf in a pond (three). I also am able to recognize a balance wheel when I see one: grandchildren. The ultimate drama is watching their variety and possibility, any children . . . the transformation of cell to flesh, limb, heart, brain—a new creature suddenly here! Itself! Original!

The noise of grandchildren growing before your eyes can make bones rattle and nerves die long before they should. Again, I am of two minds. Leave them to me and I will make them beauty itself, loving, innocent, perfect, because I am an elder and wise. No! Bring them to me at bedtime, all scrubbed and sleepy, for a good-night kiss; I want nothing to do with the rest! Why should I? I am an elder, crotchety, hoary, old, and tired *(only* when grandchildren, the future voters of the twenty-first century, come to visit like a traveling circus of lion-tamers, jugglers, and clowns.

Willow was right. I'm too critical, old-fashioned. I don't like *instantaneous,* the fastest, sharpest, the most per second, per press of the button, key, mode, robot. I worry: Will *innocence* slide off the dictionary page because of the me-me, outrageous push-iness, and greed of *instantaneous?* No generation has known so much too soon as has our grandchildren's.

"What will they do with it?" I mumble like an old hag in front of a ruined temple. "Watch out for the tender, new souls!" I warn. "No more silicone, blown up, sado-masochistic nudes in black lace garters on the walls of newspaper stands! Clear-eyed children walk there! No evening news before a child is ten! There is no love on the evening news; it's the mass unconscious in a prison breakout! Too much too soon about the Fu-ries—it can make a nine-year-old crawl out of bed in the morning like a desiccated old roué hung over from a surfeit of images! The madness of have-ness! The horses are wild! Consider!"

Consider what every generation has done

since the industrial revolution: Forests coming down, fish falling to the bottom of the sea, plants gasping for breath; now half the world intoning common prayer for ecological sanity, while the other half is deaf, bent on madness. The world is a rotting place, even with those yelling in the streets, "Make an avalanche of Right!" "Murder evil with the Truth!" "Truth is more powerful than a bullet to the brain!"

I remember expressing such thoughts to my Uncle Zachariah when he was ninety and Benjamin, our first grandchild, was two. (Little did we imagine that we would have three more, or that the Berlin Wall would come tumbling down; or that most of Eastern Europe would have taken to the streets, yelling for the Truth.)

Uncle Zachariah had laughed. "I must be younger than you. You're impassioned but depressed. I'm an optimist. Do you know why? I'll tell you. . . .

"You think a man stood in the middle of a square in Florence, Italy, in the sixteenth century and shouted, 'This is the Renaissance!'? How could he know? So how can you know that your Age and your grandchildren's will be the Age of Successful Revolution? You mark my words, I never thought I would live long enough to see it, but everyone, from a Pygmy to an Eskimo, is becoming intelligent, everyone is hearing and reading, and they want to *know.*

"The whole world is in a state of agitation, revolt, either thinking about it or doing it— to find the truth. The word *is* getting around. . . .

"My dear little girl, history is a pavane, even if, sometimes, it seems like a dervish. You have to be patient. It's God's trick that we never get the whole picture; otherwise we'd be as smart as He thinks He is, and He doesn't like that. . . . Didn't He tell us so, in the Garden, with His big, fascist voice? But I think He's changing His mind a little."

"You're naive, Uncle Zachariah," I dared to say to a ninety-year-old man.

"Intelligence will out, you baby! I have to say that until the sun gets cold or I die first. We have a lot of time. Suns are not supposed to wear out so soon. Until then, life is committed to feed on death and grow better with every bite. That's the Master's plan, no?

That's why we can always, somehow, outlive our grief and tears. . . .

"You know," he went on, "don't laugh, but I started to write a poem the other day. I haven't written one in forty years. What got into me, I don't know. . . ." He paused. "I do know. When you're close to death, it's a good idea to write a poem. Mine is about sound. You think light came first? Maybe for God, but not for Man. Not in your mother's belly. In there, sound comes first. Thump, thump, or maybe plop, plop goes the heart of your first love. And when you get out? You can't see, so light is not that special, but you hear your voice and the voices of others. Your voice is your only weapon. If you have people around you who listen with their hearts, you're lucky. If you're healthy, you're double lucky. . . ." (I could hear papers rustling over the phone; he was reading to me, not talking.) "You become a shouter. I want! I feel! I thirst!

"Waiting is an infant's cross. Some people are infants forever; they wait and wait. You discover early that you are a victim, a prisoner, first of your parents, then of the world. Unless you are a shouter. A shouter can turn

into many things: a builder of bridges . . .
or a rich man . . . or an exploiter. Or an
artist! Someone who has a song to sing for
everyone to hear. You see? Sound. The human world is nothing but one gigantic ear
waiting for messages. The natural world
couldn't care less. What does it know from
good and evil? It only knows noise. . . .

"The job is: to make a good sound, so the
human world can learn the difference. Everyone is an artist when they make a good
sound, loud and clear, in their lives. I am an
old man who was too quiet."

"Not today, you're not," I said.

Remembering his words, I am prodded to
reason like Athena, not like an old hag in
front of her ruined temple. It is not our right
to imagine there would be no glorious possibilities of sound waiting to be made by
beautiful children when they take command
of the wonders in *their* Time . . . if we have
taught them the beginnings of how.

So bring them to us elders at any time, not
only scrubbed and sweet but also sassy, curious, grimy, tearful, screaming, tantrumy,
sulking, excelling for praise, competing for
recognition, feeling poisonous thought for

the first time and being mystified by its power, not against strangers but the ones they love. Bring them to us in all their young humanity. We elders must *intrude* on the children, with intelligence and love. It is the only hope. Hope, that sublime ability possessed only by humans, to imagine and create the future.

Returning to the Light

WILLOW dared to say and do anything she wanted in her growing-old days.

Damn, damn, she banged her tiny paws against her empty plate not filled on time or enough, according to her. It was shocking. Never in all our years together, and it was going on twenty-one, had I heard one obscenity soil her lips. Now they were coming out of her lacy, pursed-up mouth, followed by gray laughs. If it weren't so sad, it would have made me laugh, because she had always been offended by my occasional *shits* and *fucks* and *goddamns*. Always a frown and the ears laid back from my tone, a little lecture about the impurity of language, the use of angry words to describe healthy functions, the Absolute Peaceful Hand. In her in-and-out-of-focus senility, she had gone back to the dank cellar talk she had most likely heard in her infancy—the unbridled and the vulgar, the animal-flailing dumb. She began to throw up a lot, she knew she was getting caught in senile lapses of dementia after a lifetime of trying to approach the Apollonian of spirit—purity, beauty, balance.

The same thing had happened to Jules's mother, that little tightly ruffled Victorian lady who clicked her tongue against her teeth because I didn't wear white gloves or a hat, I wore pleated skirts and knee socks and needed the wind in my hair. When she was on her deathbed, raving and going, Jules had brought her a dozen roses. She looked at them, turned her head away, and said, "Stick 'em up your ass." She was that angry with *dying*.

Suddenly, one day, it happened. We had to rush Willow to the nearest doctor. She was in respiratory distress. The young vet had never treated a twenty-one-year-old feline before, he said, nervous and tentative. Because Willow stood on the examining table and stared. He'd never been stared at by a cat that way before.

Our hearts plopped. "Do something, for God's sake!"

It appeared that in spite of her obsessive eating and drinking, she was in a state of extreme dehydration.

He posed a guess: "Nothing must be working."

We should have grabbed her up and raced her to her own doctor, or should we have? Could she have taken the hysteria, the quick movements, the traffic sounds? We looked at her trembling little body on the examining table and decided no. She agreed. All senility had disappeared. She was herself; her eyes pierced us with the command: "Stay!"

He filled her with fluid; syringes of it went into her miniature thighs, and she allowed it without a whimper. Anything, to live. This was too real; the mystery later was the fearful. Couldn't we see that it almost didn't matter what was done? She was going, but let's try.

We carried her home, hugging her in four

arms, and put her on a bed. Engorged with liquid, she wet herself for the first time in her life. Mortified, she pleaded forgiveness, and we pleaded with her to be forgiven. We were at a loss at how to help her.

The vet had said, did we know she was running a very high fever? "Take her home and see. . . ."

What we saw, as she curled up against a pillow, was that her opal eyes had veils over them, but they were talking: If this is the last time I can speak, remember me as I was, tried to be—proud, graceful, a collector of treasures. Suddenly she opened her eyes wide and flung away the veils. Her eyes were filled with fear, her breath was coming short. "What's happening to me? Am I dying? Tell me the truth! I demand the truth!" She slowly sank back into the beginning of coma, skeins of her awareness rolling inward.

Jules and I looked at each other. Nothing to do but rush her to a hospital for emergency treatment. Jules wrapped her in a soft towel and went to find a taxi. There was no need for a carrying case, and he wanted to hold her close. I couldn't face it. I was a coward.

They left at eleven in the evening. Jules called me an hour later. She had already been examined and was now in a deep sleep in his arms. The doctor had said her old kidneys had gone down to the size of peas. They could put her into intensive care, all hooked up, but he didn't see the point, she was an old, old lady and it was kinder to let her slip away quietly. They would begin extreme measures, if we wanted. . . . Jules said the doctor had been thoughtful and tender with her, marveling at her longevity, her tininess, and they both agreed it should be the end. Did I?

"Think it over," he said. "I'll call you back."

My father had had a slow, painful death on a respirator. Elizabeth had died a wild, disbelieving death, every nerve breaking down, on a respirator. "Let her go," I said when Jules called back. His voice was spent and sad, I could barely hear him. "Where is she?" I asked.

"Still on my lap, but she's out of it."

"Let her go, help her go," I said, hung up, and burst into tears.

When he got home, Jules told me how he

had handed her to the doctor, how the doctor had taken her gently. Jules had kissed her forehead and the doctor had suggested he observe the injection so that we would know she went quickly and humanely.

I broke down for all the loves who were no more. I cried my heart wide open for the shriveled little being who was no more. I cried for my cowardice.

Jules's hand was on my shoulder. "She knew what you could and couldn't do, she knew you so well," he said, trying to comfort me. "It didn't matter that you weren't there. She was almost out of it most of the time. . . ."

"What do you mean, *almost?*"

"While she was on my lap, she began to purr, and then gave a huge sigh, as if she were in a deep dream, it was very strange." He said the sigh was so complete, it sounded as if she were communicating from the depths of her being.

I had heard her! "I'm returning to the Light that becomes matter, to the Eternal Changes. Put mirrors on my eyes to ensure clear vision, and a jewel on my tongue for the blessed speech of animals. My heart is not pure yet, but I tried. I'm not proud of my treatment of the little bastard. . . . The best Time to die is when the sun is in the northeast. I'm dying in the middle of the night; it's not the best Time to go toward Eternal Peace. There will have to be another go-round, another Time. But I did try in this one, in a long piece of Life. Oh, it's so hard to love without shadows. . . ."

Jules said that after she had given that huge sigh, her claws dug into his knees as if to transmit, "I'm telling you something; listen well!" . . . and then she released her claws very slowly, relaxed her whole body, and he knew she wasn't there anymore.

I know she said what she did. I could hear her at home while I was crying, after I had said, "Let her go."

After Willow died, Kelly moaned for days.

Even a year later, when Kelly walked into a room, he would first look for her in her favorite places. He *never* sat in the lady's chair. As far as he was concerned, the lady's chair was occupied.